## PRAISE FOR NATHAN FLEMING &
## *PATHWAYS TO POPULATION HEALTH*

"At a time when finding a pathway forward in medical care in the U.S. is bound up in political battles, Dr. Fleming gives a clarion call to focus on public health where cooperation between agencies and health providers can address community health needs in a cost effective, efficient way. Especially in under-served, high-risk populations, empowering families to make wise choices can improve their life trajectories while reducing future health care costs."

**Dr. Ken Kihlstrom, PhD**
*Westmont College*

"*Pathways to Population Health* offers readers an insightful look into the future of public health and community financing structures for both well-versed public health professionals and those new to the field. By combining relevant examples and evidence-inspired frameworks, *Pathways to Population Health* inspires public health beginners and experts to build healthier communities. By the end of the book, readers have a renewed sense of community, collaboration, and hope for the future of public health."

**Lucas Zellmer**
*Project Coordinator, St. Clare Health Mission*

"*Pathways to Population Health* provides an important framework to move public health forward for effective community initiatives. The book delivers valuable context in policy, health care systems, provider perspectives, and community factors to understand challenges and develop solutions. Fleming addresses current issues in a pragmatic manner that will help individuals move from theory into real world implementation. He deftly connects large-scale problems to specific, focused examples that will help others who want to effect change at the local, regional, or national level. This type of approach is desperately needed to realign our resources into community-informed goals."

**Jerry Rushton, MD, MPH**
*Associate Professor of Pediatrics, Riley Hospital for Children*

"*Pathways to Population Health* is a well-reasoned discussion of the current problems facing our healthcare system with some insight from experience on a community based approach to eradicating redundancies and improving local population health. Dr. Fleming's book provides practical suggestions to help move away from irresponsible social spending and toward a low-cost, high-yield healthcare system. I would recommend this book to community leaders interested in making an impact on their own local community's healthcare."

**Kyle Rock, MD**
*Community Pediatrician*

"Dr. Fleming's work fills a gaping void in the literature describing exciting approaches to the challenging work of improving public health. His focus on engagement at the local level and directing community resources through the lens of personal experience makes [this book] especially accessible and relatable—a valuable resource for professionals and lay people alike."

**Daniel Kim, MD**
*Kaiser Permanente*

"Poor community health and preventive care wastes lives and resources on an enormous scale. For those who want to engage with these issues but want practical help and inspiration, Nathan Fleming has written the perfect book."

**Aaron RGS Hess, MD, PhD**
*University of Wisconsin-Madison*

"*Pathways to Population Health* is an insightful look into community health issues and accessibility of health services to individuals and families in need. What I loved most about this book was how, through the grace of individuals, families will have better ways to access available health services within a community. I recommend this book to individuals within a community with hopes of improving the overall betterment of family healthcare, while getting those resources to them in efficient and effective ways."

**Alex Ebben**
*Emergency Medical Technician*

"If you are working or living in a community that has silos and service gaps between healthcare and social services, then gathering resources and aligning community efforts is the answer and this book is a great place to start! Working together, we can achieve better health for all people where we live, work, learn, and play!"

**Jen Rombalski, RN, MPH**
*Health Director, La Crosse County*

# PATHWAYS TO
# POPULATION HEALTH

# PATHWAYS TO
# POPULATION
# HEALTH

## GATHER RESOURCES,
## ALIGN COMMUNITY EFFORTS,
## AND BUILD HEALTHY COMMUNITIES

## NATHAN FLEMING, MD MPH

Published by Advantage, Charleston, South Carolina.
Member of Advantage Media Group.

ADVANTAGE is a registered trademark, and the Advantage colophon is a trademark of Advantage Media Group, Inc.

Printed in the United States of America.

10  9  8  7  6  5  4  3  2  1

ISBN: 978-1-59932-838-6
LCCN: 2017958105

Cover design by George Stevens.
Layout design by Megan Elger.

This publication is designed to provide accurate and authoritative information in regard to the subject matter covered. It is sold with the understanding that the publisher is not engaged in rendering legal, accounting, or other professional services. If legal advice or other expert assistance is required, the services of a competent professional person should be sought.

Advantage Media Group is proud to be a part of the Tree Neutral® program. Tree Neutral offsets the number of trees consumed in the production and printing of this book by taking proactive steps such as planting trees in direct proportion to the number of trees used to print books. To learn more about Tree Neutral, please visit **www.treeneutral.com.**

Advantage Media Group is a publisher of business, self-improvement, and professional development books. We help entrepreneurs, business leaders, and professionals share their Stories, Passion, and Knowledge to help others Learn & Grow. Do you have a manuscript or book idea that you would like us to consider for publishing? Please visit advantagefamily.com or call **1.866.775.1696.**

*To Jim and Barbara Fleming.*

# TABLE OF CONTENTS

Healthcare alone cannot finance and deliver better health outcomes. We have the opportunity to transform community health through cross-sector collaboration. If we gather resources, align community efforts, and focus on social factors driving medical outcomes, then we can improve population health. Collaboration between local government, public health, healthcare systems, nonprofits, and social service agencies can transform population health outcomes.

# BUILDING HEALTHY COMMUNITIES

**CHALLENGE:** *The design of our towns makes it hard for families to be healthy. Can we design our communities to make healthy choices easy for families?*

# LIST OF FIGURES

## LIST OF TABLES

# FOREWORD

I had heard tales of Dr. Fleming from colleagues, here in La Crosse, months before I met him. Most stories seemed like a mixture of truth and lore: an MD going door to door in southern India collecting stool samples as part of his Harvard coursework, explaining through a translator that he, a doctor arriving in a suit adorned with a flowered lapel, was there because he needed a little of their poop. Families started calling him Dr. Poo. He later told me that he wore the flower so that he and community members could smell something sweet while discussing and dealing in something so odorous. The goal was to always be kind and graceful and promote dignity, even when discussing diarrhea.

Dr. Fleming opted not to work as a pediatrician but instead as a population health consultant in one of our local healthcare institutions, foregoing a large salary for a more impassioned existence. Dr. Fleming would negotiate with his superiors, as he was often a bit backed up on the assigned work because he was so busy doing work that would ultimately prove more meaningful and important to both the healthcare organization and our community. As with all passionate people, Dr. Fleming was a joy to work with 90 percent of the time. The other 10 percent of the time, Nathan was challenging us to take risks and bold actions that tend to make a person wholly uncomfortable. But those risks ultimately will prove to yield great results for our community.

In my career, I have worked with and for funders, county governments, and nonprofits. All have their unique challenges and frustrations. Often, funding goes to the latest and most exciting projects rather than to projects that are proven to work. We treat programs, tasked with moving our community forward, in a similar fashion as we treat new cell phones— we must have the latest, flashiest, and most popular. Often, what works takes a back seat to our communities' excitement about something "new." A few years later, we start over again, with a new exciting product promising to be the magic bullet in human services or healthcare. In county governments, change is stymied by bureaucracy, where the best educated and trained social workers are reduced to brokers of services and data entry clerks mandated by ineffective polices at the state and federal level. In nonprofits, there are also the haves and have-nots; the funding game can be likened to The Hunger Games for adults. It takes new thinking and a complex systems approach to solve the problems of our time.

Dr. Fleming has devoted his education and career to serving those without a voice, whether as a pediatrician or working tirelessly for population health initiatives in developing countries, rural counties, clinics, or as a Harvard trained population health consultant. What Dr. Fleming proposed for our community was not the latest, greatest, or flashiest—it was a coupling of promising and proven programs and strategies from around the nation with existing programs and funding to solve real problems for real people struggling in our community. From meeting Dr. Fleming in a local coffee shop to now reading this important work, he is a gift to the communities he serves.

**Jason Larsen, MBA**
Executive Director, Big Brothers Big Sisters of the 7 Rivers Region

# POPULATION HEALTH UNDERGROUND

**CHALLENGE:** $1,000,000 for Population Health

*"Wouldn't it be nice to have a million dollars to address social needs?"*

—Sandy Brekke, director, St. Clare Health Mission

## STARTING IN A COFFEE SHOP

A pediatrician, college student, therapist, professor, county health director, and free clinic director meet at a coffee shop, and the community gives them $650,000 to improve population health.

Sounds ridiculous, right? It must be a joke, because that couldn't possibly happen . . . well, it happened in February 2017.

It started when three friends decided to get coffee on a Friday afternoon. It turns out, no one schedules meetings on Friday afternoon. So, we were each able to block the time, and tell our respective bosses that we were working on "community collaboration." However, we knew our bosses would not look kindly on fraternizing with the enemy. Two of us were employed by rival healthcare systems. Luc started his own nonprofit, Wheels-for-All, that builds bicycles for the homeless. He then became the volunteer coordinator of the community free clinic. We needed to keep a low profile and we worked in the shadows to avoid "The Man."

We had our own code for how we would protect our time. Sandy labeled it as "FYF," I marked the calendar as "GSD," and Luc's Google calendar said, "Coffee." FYF stands for "Find Your Freedom." It's inspirational. GSD means "Get 'Stuff' Done." And Coffee means Coffee. Luc is the only truly honest man in the group. We would sit at a coffee shop and brainstorm how to improve our respective organizations through collaboration.

## COFFEE SHOP TALK—THE POWER OF THIRD SPACES TO CHANGE THE WORLD

Soon, we were having fun and making progress. During the week, we could help each other connect families and clients to resources. Then Jason joined the group. He heard about coffee on Fridays from Sandy.

Jason worked for the County Human Services Department and ran La Crosse Family Collaborative. The La Crosse Family Collaborative embedded social workers in high-risk neighborhoods to provide early interventions for struggling families. The idea was to keep kids safe by addressing unmet needs early. The goal was to reduce the need for child protective services by preventing abuse and neglect. Jason had awesome ideas!

Then Sarah and Matthew joined. Sarah has a brightly dyed swatch of hair, and Matthew is lean and serious. Sarah is a PhD therapist who runs the YMCA Teen Center, a safe place for adolescents to go after school, relax, make art, and build healthy relationships. Matthew is a professor at Viterbo, the local liberal arts university. His dissertation focused on the intersection of theology, religion, and global health in the primary healthcare movement and the response to the AIDS pandemic. Sarah is fun/spontaneous; Matthew is fun/serious. The contrasting styles made the group stronger.

Then the County Health Director, Jen, started coming. Soon, we were taking over multiple tables. The ideas emerged naturally as we shared stories, collaborated on grants, and tried new things "on the down low." It was so much fun.

Our first attempt to collaborate failed. We tried to apply for a Robert Wood Johnson Foundation (RWJF) Culture of Health Leadership grant. RJWF trains and equips local leaders to implement a culture of health. The application is competitive, and you have to submit a short video explaining how a culture of health will improve your community. We made a video together—it was low budget and terrible. The application—honestly—was raw and messy. We didn't have most of the institutional supports that RJWF looks for when they invest in local leaders. But everyone at the coffee shop on Friday learned that we loved to work together and it was life giving to collaborate across organizations with a shared vision for our community.

The first big win was when Jen committed the county health department to adopt a five-year strategic plan that addressed the social determinants of health. We did not need an official title or external funding to start building a population health effort that connected resources and coordinated efforts across all our organizations. We could start addressing the upstream social factors that drive health outcomes using existing programs in our neighborhoods. When La Crosse County revised the County Health Improvement Plan, Jen made some strategic decisions. The County Health Department committed "to create social and physical environments that promote good health for all" and outlined measurable objectives to "ensure a system exists to connect people in need with available resources" by December 2021. Our coffee shop talk was now La Crosse County policy!

## PRIORITY AREA – SOCIAL DETERMINANTS

**GOAL:** To create social and physical environments that promote good health for all.

### PERFORMANCE MEASURES

| OBJECTIVE | INDICATORS OR MEASURES (LIST SOURCE) *Indicators are the data trends. They are not intended to be measures of success. |
|---|---|
| By December 31, 2021, assure that a system exists that connects people in need to available resources in La Crosse County. | Percent of adults 18 years and over who report not receiving sufficient social-emotional support (BRFSS) Community perception of health, safety, education, quality of life, and economic aspects as well as access to care (COMPASS) Calls for resources related to social determinants (211 Call Data) |

### ALIGNMENT

| LCHD CHA | Healthiest Wisconsin 2020 | Healthy People 2020 |
|---|---|---|
| Social determinants was rated as the third highest concern in the La Crosse County Health Department Community Health Assessment which included data from the COMPASS NOW 2015 survey, key informant interviews, community forums, and community leader rankings. | Health Literacy Objective 2: By 2020, increase effective communication so that individuals, organizations, and communities can access, understand, share and act on health information and services. | (ASH-6.1) Reduce the proportion of persons who are unable to obtain necessary medical care, dental care, or prescription medicines. |

OBJECTIVE: BY DECEMBER 31, 2021, ASSURE THAT A SYSTEM EXISTS THAT CONNECTS PEOPLE IN NEED TO AVAILABLE RESOURCES.

**Public Health**

**FIGURE 1.1. Community Health Improvement Plan (CHIP)**

*A community health improvement plan uses local data to identify priority issues, implement strategies for action, and measure community-wide improvement. A CHIP broadly imagines the way in which the activities of many organizations contribute to population health. La Crosse County Health Department decided to prioritize social determinants of health and leverage existing resources to promote health for everyone in the community.*

By the county health department embracing the vision, it provided a clear direction and mission for the group to push forward. Jen was the leader and champion who convened and influenced community partners.

Eventually, we were able to put together a business plan on how to improve care coordination across community agencies. We found evidence-based models and local sources of waste and duplication. We had figured out how to make life easier for the healthcare systems, the county health department, the local United Way, and the free clinic. The pitch was compelling, and more and more people wanted to participate.

## POPULATION HEALTH UNDERGROUND

At this point, our Friday coffee group had taken on an unofficial–official title: the Population Health Underground. Given our unofficial–official status, we invited Health Leads USA to run a workshop consisting of six structured discussions focused on:

- social needs programs
- choosing social needs and designing interventions
- patient population and screening
- workforce considerations
- measuring quality and impact
- enhancing social needs programs in our hometown

The group at Health Leads USA,[1] Rich Porcelli and the entire team, were phenomenal. If you ever have the chance to participate, either as an individual or organization, in the Health Leads "Preparing to Build a Social Needs Program" workshop, I would highly recommend it.

Rather than do the workshop as a group of friends with shared interests, we decided to invite frontline workers from key organizations and sectors throughout the community. We had peers from the school district, county health department, Age and Disability Resource Center, YMCA Teen Center, the Health Science Consortium (support organization for higher education in the community), Health System Social Workers, United Way Outreach Coordinators, 221 Referral Line, and Community Foundation. The talent as well as the boots-on-the-ground knowledge was staggering. Rather than start with the end in mind, we focused on the data:

- What are the most pressing social needs in our community?

- Who can we partner with?

- How should we measure our efforts?

But given our unofficial–official status and the number of participants, we needed to find a meeting space large enough for everyone to be at the same table. We also wanted to avoid meeting at a health institution—such as a hospital or county office—because the goal was to have a community-run, community-owned collaboration. Great Rivers United Way let us use their basement. Local chapters of the United Way can be great conveners of community stakeholders. Great Rivers United Way works to create opportunities for a better life for everyone. Their website describes the mission and vision of the staff:

*Advancing the common good is less about helping one person at a time and more about changing systems to help all of us. We are all connected and interdependent. We all win when a child succeeds in school, when families are financially stable, when people are healthy. United Way's goal is to create long-lasting changes in the region by addressing the underlying causes of these problems. Living united means being a part of the change. It takes everyone in our community working together to create a brighter future.[2]*

At first, it was a fairly routine community meeting in the basement of a building. But, friends were made, and the coffee shop group coalesced into a full-blown community collaboration. People were staying after the meetings ended to connect, chat, and coordinate efforts across organizations. Meetings were being scheduled to start before or after to pull in additional participants. Connections were being made to other initiatives and new programs.

We all recognized that our county had a wealth of resources to support vulnerable families: two medical systems; three college/universities; government initiatives on education, housing, homelessness, addiction and employment; a socially conscious business community; and nonprofits and generous community foundations.

At the end of six weeks, frontline workers for thirteen community agencies came to together and articulated a plan for our community that we could each share—in our own words and in ways that our bosses would appreciate. For the group in La Crosse in the summer of 2016, the result looked like this:

*Social Determinants of Health are the major drivers of health-care outcomes. We will elevate the health of the community by partnering with service providers, investing in relationships, and accelerating community transformations towards justice, supportive, bi-directional systems of caring. If we can go upstream and intervene early, then we break the cycle of poverty and enhance the health and wellbeing of our communities while enriching every life we touch.*

*The GRACE FOR LA CROSSE collaboration brings together disparate sectors to align around a vision for a better community, enhance existing programs, and unlock new sources of investment in the most vulnerable neighborhoods. By improving links between existing programs, providing screening, navigation, and referral services to vulnerable families, and reimbursing agencies for both screening community members and completing evidence-based interventions, we will improve health outcomes across our city.*

*We hope to build lasting relationships in our neighborhoods that extend beyond the scope of the collaboration and accelerate the work of other community initiatives. Our potential solutions will inform the regional conversation about how to best invest to achieve health equity in more communities throughout the Great Rivers area. We can harness community interest, current technology, and existing data to catalyze change, beginning with an evidence-based understanding of the problem and continuing to measure data for assessing impact.*[3]

In addition to the inspiration vision statement, we mapped the services provided throughout the county by healthcare organizations, county government agencies, and nonprofits. The resulting spreadsheet—printed out—was almost twenty pages long and categorized programs by social determinants. In all, we had more than three hundred programs targeting nutrition, exercise, housing, parenting, transportation, green spaces, elder care, home visits, violence prevention, safe neighborhoods, and more than forty different categories of services.

When the local paper covered the story, there were no mentions of coffee shops, population health underground, or references to basement discussions. In fact, it was the community leaders who were interviewed. The leadership had been inspired to lead the change that was presented by the lowly groundlings discussing how to build or enhance social needs programs over lunch in the basement of United Way.

As you can see, La Crosse already had a critical mass of frontline workers interested in collaboration. But it took time, patience, and coordination between multiple community agencies to identify the partners, patterns, and connections that would enable easy navigation for families. It was amazing what happened when frontline works from healthcare systems, Aging and Disability Resource Center, YMCA, the county health department, the community-run free clinic, 211 Resource Directory, and Community Foundation worked together to enhance social needs programs.

## PAYING FOR HEALTH—THE US LANDSCAPE

The American healthcare system is a high-cost, low-yield investment. Despite spending nearly 50 percent more per capita than most developed countries, the United States ranks just above the median in health outcomes when compared to other industrialized nations.[4] David Kindig, a physician and PhD economist, opens his landmark book, *Purchasing Population Health*, with this observation: "While we [Americans] are global leaders in technical accomplishments in medicine, the amount of health we achieve per dollar is invested far from optimal." In short, we have money and we have technology, but we don't allocate either very well. He concludes his book:

> *Population health improvement will not be achieved until appropriate incentives are designed. . . . Simply put, implementing an approach to measure and pay for cost-effective improvement in population health status is the best opportunity we have for bringing value to U.S. patients and purchasers.*[5]

Kindig wrote his book in 1997 during the tumultuous healthcare reforms of the 1990s. He believed the United States would adequately fund population health "in the next 25 years." It is now 2017, almost twenty years later, and I am writing a book on how to help communities pay for population health.

How are we going to make more progress in the next five years than has been accomplished in the last twenty? I think we are in a position to transform healthcare from a high-cost, low-yield investment to a low-cost, high-yield investment if we are willing to gather resources, align community efforts, address the social determinants of health, and improve population health outcomes.

As we consider how to Gather Resources and Align Community Effort (GRACE), it will be important to answer some fundamental questions about healthcare financing:

- How much money is available to pay for health?

- Do the financial incentives in healthcare align with population health priorities?

- What barriers are preventing progress on population health priorities?

How can we sort, simplify, sweep, standardize, and sustain existing programs to address the social factors driving healthcare expenses?

## SPENDING MORE AND GETTING LESS— THE US HEALTHCARE PARADOX

Here are the striking numbers about the cost of healthcare in the United States:

- We spend $3.4 trillion on healthcare every year, or about $10,350 per person (2017).

- Hospitals and clinics report $34 billion in uncompensated care every year (2016).[6]

- Private foundations spend $93 billion in the US every year to support critical social programs in the areas of community development, social services, job training, and education,[7] or around $262 per person (2011).

- The Centers for Disease Control and Prevention's (CDC) budget is $7.17 billion or about $22 per person (2016).

- State public health spending budget is around $11.5 billion total, with median spending $31 per person in each county (2016).[8]

As you watch the healthcare debates in Washington, DC, I beg you to please, please keep the scale of these numbers in mind. It is easy to confuse a million, a billion, and trillion. For instance, one of the my favorite webcomics, *XKCD*, explains the challenge of "1000x" this way:

**FIGURE 1.2. 1000x: The Difference between a Billion and a Trillion**

*When program costs are mentioned as millions, billions, or trillions, the impression left by the cited number is not some specific amount but rather some generically large amount of money. A trillion is a thousand times larger than a billion, but if one is not paying close attention, they both mentally register as being "very large" or "life-changing if they ended up in my bank account," rather than being as different as "one dollar" and "a thousand dollars" are.*[9]

The US spends a fortune on healthcare, but our system is stingy when it comes to public health and prevention:

| | |
|---|---|
| Healthcare | $3,400 billion |
| Philanthropy | $93 billion |
| Uncompensated Healthcare | $34 billion |
| County Health Budgets | $11 billion |

The difference between a trillion and billion dollars works out like this: we spend around $53 per person in public health spending, depending on what state you live in, compared to $10,350 per person in medical care spending.[10] Even more importantly, healthcare systems lose three times more money through uncompensated care than we spend, in total, on population health.

The Peterson-Kaiser Health System Tracker illustrates how the US is performing relative to other countries, and how different parts of the system are performing relative to one another.[11]

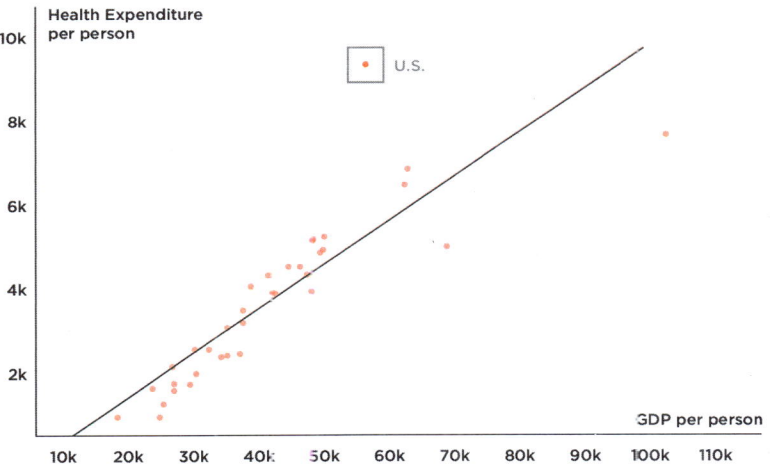

## RELATIVE TO THE SIZE OF ITS WEALTH, THE U.S. SPENDS A DISPROPORTIONATE AMOUNT ON HEALTH CARE

Total health expenditures per capita/GDP per capita, U.S. dollars, PPP adjusted, 2015

- OTHER DEVELOPED NATIONS
- UNITED STATES

**FIGURE 1.3. Wealth, Healthcare Spending, and Health**

*The US spends a huge amount on healthcare, more than every other country. Even when we adjust healthcare spending relative to individuals (per capita) the US spends a disproportionate amount on healthcare without achieving a healthier population or longer life span. You can use the Peterson-Kaiser Health System Tracker to explore links between wealth, healthcare spending, and health.*

On average, other wealthy countries spend about half as much person on healthcare as the US does, but other countries spend more on social services. The US is the only wealthy country to spend more (as a percentage of GDP) on healthcare than on the social factors that drive healthcare utilization.[12] The reality is that most public health funds, even though they are a small fraction of total healthcare spending, do not go to local public health departments.

It is not just public health spending. In a well-written, well-researched 272-page book, *The American Healthcare Paradox: Why Spending More Is Getting Us Less*, health policy experts Elizabeth Bradley and Lauren Taylor found that the US spent the least on social services—such as retirement and disability benefits, employment programs, and supportive housing—among seventeen developed countries, at just 9 percent of GDP. The US was also the only country studied where healthcare spending accounted for a greater share of GDP than social services spending.[13]

Even within the healthcare system, we do not prioritize low-cost, high-yield investments. Michael P. Pignone of the University of North Carolina-Chapel Hill explains, "Individuals with one or more chronic conditions account for approximately $1.5 trillion in healthcare spending per year." Based on Pignone's calculations, "the widespread use of effective interventions, such as disease management, post-discharge care, and case management for key chronic conditions could produce substantial savings, perhaps as much as $45 billion per year."[14] Yet we keep funneling money into medical care, instead of public health, population health, and prevention services.

Currently, the costs of poor population health are spread across a variety of community organizations: local government, healthcare systems, county health departments, health insurance programs—including Medicaid and Medicare—and businesses. Each stakeholder loses money via a different mechanism, but all lose out when we fail to address the basic needs that drive population health expenses. City and county governments lose revenues when families are unable to work. Plus, city and governments are responsible for maintaining the community safety net. The cost of treatment for addiction, homelessness, foster care, crime, and neighborhood maintenance fall on local government programs. Healthcare systems face major costs due to uncompensated care. As a part of the Affordable Care Act, healthcare systems began reporting uncompensated care and community benefit dollars in order to maintain their preferred tax status. The cost of uncompensated care typically runs in the hundreds of millions of dollars for regional health systems. Preventable hospital admissions, hospital-acquired infections, overutilization of emergency services, psychiatric services, and expensive unhealthy behaviors lead to millions of dollars in ineffective or unnecessary medical bills. Local businesses lose money when workers can't work due to health issues, absenteeism, childcare, elder care, and worker-job mismatches that limit growth and entrepreneurship.

We can break the cycle of underinvestment in better health outcomes by clearly connecting social data to medical outcomes. If we can show stakeholders how much the status quo costs and how little health their money is buying, then we can make progress toward population health. We will pay for population health by encouraging local leaders to invest in the health and well-being of the community.

The challenge is not just who will pay but also how to ensure that the community money is well spent. Current systems and structures for funding population health are broken. The financing is short term and disconnected from community outcomes.

## HEALTHCARE TODAY VERSUS POPULATION HEALTH FOR TOMORROW

Everyone in the Population Health Underground felt that the current system for financing and coordinating care in La Crosse was broken.

We wanted to work in partnership across government, health, and nonprofit sectors to create a system of care coordination that would connect young children, families, and seniors to social supports. The goal was to empower high-risk families to take coordinated, step-by-step actions toward achieving their goals for a positive life trajectory.

The members of the Population Health Underground had a front-row, first-person view of our healthcare system. Healthcare is great at treating disease for people with insurance and those individuals savvy enough to navigate the system. However, it was a Kafka-esque nightmare for struggling families. We all thought that if we could pool resources, expertise, and staff to effectively address the most common social needs, then we would have a new system that supported health, not merely triaged and treated disease. We collectively acknowledged that unmet social needs—housing insecurity, financial resource strain, transportation, exposure to violence, child care, education, employment, social isolation, and behavioral health—were the major drivers of health outcomes in our community.

POPULATION HEALTH UNDERGROUND CREATED A SAFE SPACE, A LOCAL COFFEE SHOP FOR FRONTLINE WORKERS TO DISCUSS PROBLEMS AND SHARE SOLUTIONS TO HELP FAMILIES AND ORGANIZATIONS IN OUR COMMUNITY.

| CARE PROCESS | TODAY'S HEALTHCARE | FUTURE POPULATION HEALTH | BENEFIT |
|---|---|---|---|
| IDENTIFICATION OF UNMET SOCIAL NEEDS | Ad hoc, depending on whether community member raises concerns during an encounter with healthcare or social services system | Systematic screening of all vulnerable communities members, including at-risk families and isolated seniors | Systematic screening provides better information on risk to healthcare and social service providers and avoids duplicated efforts across the care continuum |
| PROVIDER RESPONSE TO UNMET SOCIAL NEEDS | Ad hoc, depending on whether the provider is aware of resources in the community | Systematic connections to community services through intensive care coordination and community resource navigation | Community members are connected quickly and directly to service organizations best positioned to address their needs, eliminating wasted effort and confusion |
| AVAILABILITY OF SUPPORT TO HELP COMMUNITY MEMBERS RESOLVE UNMET SOCIAL NEEDS | Ad hoc, depending on whether case manager is available and has capacity, given case load and care coordination responsibilities | Community Care Coordination designed to help at-risk families overcome barriers to accessing services | Front-line workers benefit from a robust infrastructure to support care coordination including tracking, reporting, and billing integrated into existing workflows |
| AVAILABILITY OF COMMUNITY SERVICES TO ADDRESS UNMET SOCIAL NEEDS | Dependent on fragmented community service system not aligned with needs of families and seniors, often resulting in waitlist, confusion, and frustration | Aligned social services, data-driven continuous quality improvement and community collaborations to assess and build service capacity | Better, timely, effective services for community members. Care coordinators focus on serving the community, not servicing the system. Aggregated, high-quality data from multiple agencies to demonstrate impact to funders and stakeholders |
| FINANCING OF SERVICES AT COMMUNITY AGENCIES | 1. Grants—typically from community, state, and regional foundations; 2. Public contacts funded by tax levy and determined by state and county budgets | Pay-for-outcomes social services. Contracts with business and health insurance plans pay community providers when families thrive and unmet social needs are addressed. | 1. Families are better served by coordinated systems. 2. Provider agencies are freed from an endless grant seeking cycle. 3. Community service agencies focus on their core mission: Helping at-risk families thrive 4. Community benefit $$ clearly connected to collective impact |

**TABLE 1.1. Population Health Underground Promotes Health for Today and Tomorrow**

*The advantage of meeting informally in coffee shops is that it allows for a low-risk, low-stress environment to complain about the way things are and imagine a community that is better. There are significant differences in healthcare and population health in*

*identifying unmet needs, supporting providers, solving problems for clients, connecting community services, and paying for social needs programs. Coffee shop talk provides a safe space to learn how to articulate problems with healthcare and to explain the benefits of a community-based population health approach.*

The Population Health Underground believed that prioritizing population health would help our community—La Crosse County—transform population health, save payers money, and empower social workers, public health nurses, and community health workers to promote health where people live, work, learn, play, age, worship, and relax.

Our goal was a population health collaboration that:

- Systematically screened families to identify unmet social needs. Screening results are made available to all providers working with a single household.

- Tested the effectiveness of referrals using standardized pathways with clear incentives to providers. Pathways help community members rapidly and effectively resolve unmet social needs.

- Shifted the focus from reactionary care to preventative care to improve ongoing health and, therefore, lower overall costs. A focus on preventative care would help organizations in La Crosse leverage individual and family involvement in health and prevention, improving medication compliance, and tracking outcomes so that you have verified proof that the criteria for success—and reimbursement—are met.

- Streamlined management of community member information reduces duplication of services (and costs), while encouraging a team approach to health and healthcare that improves communication between providers and human services systems—and enhances the efficiency of providing appropriate care.

- Sustainably financed social services to support infrastructure capacity building, workforce training, and collective impact Hubs can help communities reduce spending and realize results by connecting to communities.

- Aligned the activities of service providers at the community level to strategically utilize existing resources and implement quality improvement approaches to eliminate waste and assist community members in overcoming barriers to access and to completion of social programs.

We had a lot of goals, but we did not have a clear message that spoke to the mission and vision of the group.

## GRACE WAS BORN IN THE POPULATION UNDERGROUND

As we discussed our goals and vision, we kept coming back to the concept of "Grace." Grace, in the Judeo-Christian tradition, represents "the free and unmerited favor of God, as manifested in the bestowal of blessings." It is a free gift, given not earned, that helps struggling individuals to thrive. We wanted to be a blessing for our community. We wanted to be present in the daily struggles of working families. Grace—the theological concept—encapsulated the abstract concept that was missing from our healthcare system.

Now, I need to tell you a little bit about me. I love Scrabble, acronyms, puzzles, and memes. I started to try to figure out how we could repurpose the word "G-R-A-C-E" to explain our mission and vision for population health collaboration. After multiple attempts, we realized that GRACE could perfectly explain what we were trying to do. As a group, we wanted to:

- gather resources

- align community effort
- address the social factors driving medical outcomes (those social determinants of health)
- improve population health

We wanted to spread GRACE around our hometown:

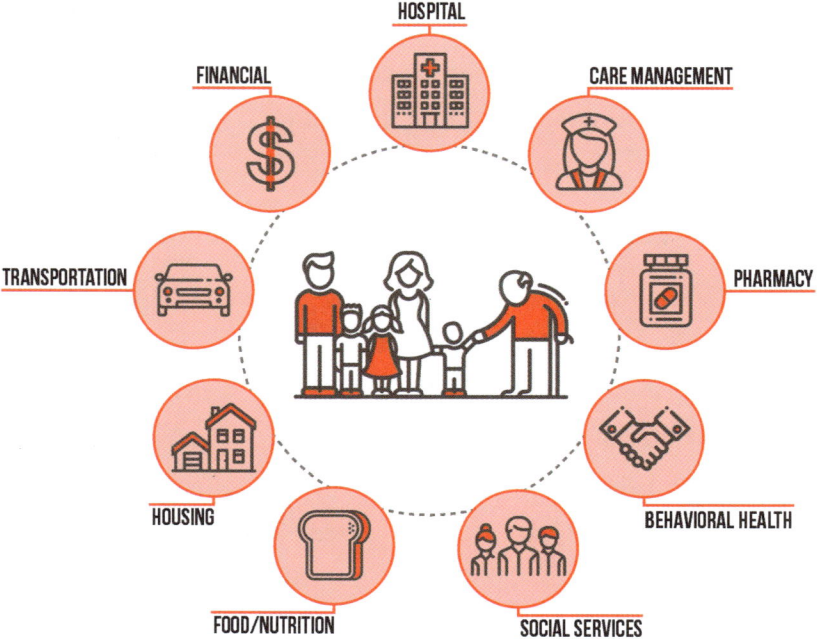

## GRACE CONNECTS SOCIAL NEEDS TO MEDICAL OUTCOMES USING PROGRAMS AND SERVICES IN THE COMMUNITY

GATHER RESOURCES + ALIGN COMMUNITY EFFORT = BUILD HEALTHIER HOMETOWNS FOR EVERYONE

 **FIGURE 1.4. GRACE (Gather Resources Align Community Effort)**

*GRACE is an unmerited gift that changes a life. The goal of Pathways to Population Health is to put families in the center of a system that listens and responds to their needs and priorities.*

Remember the Sandy Brekke challenge? One million dollars to address social needs? After the Population Health Underground embraced GRACE as a mission and visions, we were able to gather $650,000 in local funds to improve population health. It was not a million dollars, but it was a lot of new money to drive collaboration, collective impact, and better health for working families.

## REFLECTION QUESTIONS

1.  What steps can you take today to begin organizing population health in your community?

2.  How will you learn the history of your community and identify the local leaders with a shared vision, desire to collaborate, and interest in social determinants of health?

3.  Has your local health system or county health department collaborated on population health initiatives in the past? If so, can you build on that project?

4.  Determine what is the single biggest social challenge facing your community over the next five years. Would you be able to tackle it with the combined efforts of healthcare systems, public health, social services, and nonprofits?

---

**PART 1 ENDNOTES**

1   Health Leads, "Prepare Workshop," *HealthLeadsUSA.org* (n.d.), https://health-leadsusa.org/solutions/design/prepare-workshop/
2   http://www.greatriversunitedway.org
3   Mike Tighe, "Great Rivers Hub Prepares for Summer Rollout to Connect People with Services," *La Crosse Tribune,* June 3, 2017. http://lacrossetribune.com/

news/local/great-rivers-hub-prepares-for-summer-rollout-to-connect-people/
article_a01c5768-8a3b-5f03-96a4-7406c08ebcf2.html

4   Kaiser Family Foundation analysis of data from OECD (2017), "OECD Data: health
    Expenditure and Financing: Health expenditure indicators." OECD Health Statis-
    tics (Database).

5   David Kindig, *Purchasing Population Health: Paying for Results* (Ann Arbor: The
    University of Michigan Press, 1997), 174.

6   American Hospital Association, "What Is Uncompensated Care?" (December
    2016), *American Hospital Association*, www.aha.org/content/16/uncompensat-
    edcarefactsheet.pdf

7   Philanthropy Roundtable, "Real Rise in US Giving." *Philanthropy Roundtable*
    (2017) www.philanthropyroundtable.org/almanac/statistics/

8   Laura Segal and Alejandra Martin, "Investing America's Health: A State-by-
    State Look at Public Funding and Key Health Facts," *Trust for America's Health
    and Robert Wood Johnson Foundation* (2017) http://healthyamericans.org/
    report/136/

9   Original XKCD comic appears at: https://xkcd.com/558/. https://www.
    explainxkcd.com/wiki/index.php/558:_1000_Times

10  Segal and Martin.

11  Peterson-Kaiser, *Health System Tracker*, www.healthsystemtracker.org

12  Peterson-Kaiser.

13  Elizabeth Bradley and Lauren Taylor, *The American Healthcare Paradox* (New
    York: PublicAffairs, 2013).

14  P. L. Yong, R. S. Saunders, and L. A. Olsen, eds, "Missed Prevention Opportuni-
    ties," in *The Healthcare Imperative: Lowering Costs and Improving Outcomes:
    Workshop Series Summary* (Washington, DC: National Academies Press, 2010),
    www.ncbi.nlm.nih.gov/books/NBK53914/

# POPULATION HEALTH UNICORNS AND PRAIRIE DOGS

**CHALLENGE:** Systems to improve health don't work together. Can we improve health by building a culture of health in our hometowns?

The current political climate has led state and federal government to threaten to defund social safety net programs while proven interventions remain unfunded. Local systems will have to unite and share infrastructure if community safety nets are to survive. In fact, the US safety is intentionally decentralized to allow local governments the freedom to innovate, customize, and adapt national programs to local needs. → don't have to follow national norm'

Population health has gained popularity as a multidisciplinary field that connects individual efforts to community outcomes. It is more inclusive than public health or population medicine. It provides a common ground and common language for healthcare providers, public health experts, and social service workers to unite, share, and collaborate. Population health is outcomes focused and profoundly relational. It is also subversive: it up-ends the status quo.

Population health programs will challenge traditional silos and power structures. It will provide new funding streams for innovative, multidisciplinary programs. But it will pull resources away from narrowly focused, ineffective, and unproductive activities. There will be opportunities for new leaders to join the workforce. But old jobs may need to be reimagined and old workers may need to be retrained. Rather than direct these changes from the top-down, I imagine they will emerge from the bottom up. The name—Pathways to Population Health—means change will start at a grassroots level, percolate in coffee shops, spread between friends, and provide connections across institutional boundaries.

## SYSTEMS TO IMPROVE HEALTH DON'T WORK TOGETHER

My county supports multiple systems dedicated to improving health and well-being. There is a healthcare system—in fact, there are two large, integrated healthcare systems that compete to provide healthcare services. There is a public health system funded and administered by the local government. There are social services provided by businesses, local government agencies, and nonprofit organizations. There are charities and nonprofits funded by philanthropy. There are also a variety of for-profit businesses that address basic health needs. Each system—healthcare, public health, social services, charity, and commercial business—exists in its unique niche. The mission, reach, market, staff, and funding are different. But a common purpose (to improve the health and well-being of the community) and a common population (the community members they exist to serve) connect the different systems. Michael Marmot has led a generation of thinkers to evaluate the systematic and social causes of health disparities. In 2000, Marmot received a knighthood from the Queen of England for his work to help us understand health inequalities. As a giant among men who care about the health impact of social inequalities, Marmot notes, "As physicians we are trained that the patient comes first and last. Searching out individual causes of disease, however, does not negate the importance of environmental causes."[1] I believe that we are ready for a shift from systems working in silos toward a more integrative, collaborative community approach to health.

The traditional, narrow definition of healthcare that focuses on healthcare delivered by doctors in hospitals must be replaced by a more holistic definition of health and well-being that looks outside the walls of the healthcare system to address the social and environmental drivers of health and illness in the community. The nation's current trajectory of healthcare spending poses significant threats to economic development, as well as to the sustainability of healthcare systems themselves. Projected increases in population growth, retirees, and public healthcare costs, if not arrested, could pose serious challenges to maintaining critical safety net systems (Medicare, Medicaid), coping with extreme events (disease outbreaks), and safeguarding health. An unprecedented cut in healthcare spending accompanied by a dramatic improvement in health outcomes would be required to mitigate these risks; however, accomplishing that would necessitate implementation of some drastic changes in public health, healthcare systems, social services, business, education, criminal justice, philanthropy, and safety net systems. Health is an issue that presents great social, scientific, and economic complexity, some very deep uncertainties, profound ethical issues, and even a lack of agreement on what the problem is. But we—as a community—have a choice. There are new paradigms for improving population health that could avert the coming financial and health crisis.

## WHAT IS HEALTH? ~~cond highlighted this~~

Competing definitions of health lead to confusing allocations of funds to promote health. Currently, most of the money goes into healthcare, with marginal amounts of spending split between population health, population health management, population medicine, public health, community health, and personalized medicine. Healthcare tends to be the most reactionary. Healthcare systems wait for people to get sick and seek help, and then the healthcare systems treat the disease on a fee-for-service basis. The other definitions of health focus on identifying risks of developing disease, proactively addressing risk with a goal of promoting health and preventing disease. The different models go by many different names—Total Population Health, Culture of Health, Healthy People 2020, HI-5, Roadmap to Health, Building Health Communities—but because we are talking about similar ideas to achieve the same end goal, I call it: Population Health.

| WHAT IS HEALTH?—KEY TERM AS DEFINED BY VARIOUS PROFESSIONAL GROUPS | |
|---|---|
| HEALTH | A state of complete physical, mental, and social well-being, and not merely the absence of disease or infirmity (WHO) |
| HEALTHCARE | Access, utilization, and quality medical services delivered to treat disease and prevent complications (AHA) |
| POPULATION HEALTH | The health outcomes of a group of individuals, including the distribution of such outcomes within the group (Kindig) |
| POPULATION HEALTH MANAGEMENT OR POPULATION MEDICINE | When the healthcare system tackles population health issues dealing with patients, then physicians, experts, and administrators may talk about Population Health Management or Medicine. The focus is on interventions delivered to groups of patients at scale based on risk. (IHI) |
| PUBLIC HEALTH OR COMMUNITY HEALTH | The promotion and protection of health of communities through population-based interventions, policies, and health education (AFHA) |
| PERSONALIZE MEDICINE | The synthesis of big data (population health, epidemiology) with advanced diagnostics (genomics) to customize interventions to individuals' risks and tailor predicted individual responses (NIH) |

**TABLE 2.1. What Is Health?**

*There are many different ways to talk about health. It is important to define terms and understand the priorities of different organizations involved in delivering health to the community. The World Health Organization provides a very broad definition of health that sees individuals through the lens of the community outcomes; whereas the National Institute of Health defines personalized medicine and focuses on the connections between individuals and big data systems. In between, it can be helpful to remember that there is a range of definitions that move from broad to narrow: public health, population health, population health management, and healthcare.*

The World Health Organization (WHO) describes the healthcare system as a "complex network of agencies, facilities, organizations, institutions, clinics, hospitals, nursing homes, and all providers in a geographic area that deliver services, medicines, procedures, and technologies with the purpose to prevent disease, treat illness and alleviate suffering." Basically, it is all the organizations, people, and actions whose primary intent is to promote, restore, and maintain health. In the US, we have a much more restricted idea of "healthcare." Healthcare is primarily the hospitals, clinics, doctors, nurses, and medical staff who treat disease. It does not include the public health departments, social service agencies, nonprofits, and businesses

world
vs
us

in community that try to promote, restore, and maintain health. For instance, we typically don't think of policemen as health officers— but law enforcement has a huge role in keeping families safe and healthy. Nor would you consider your garbage man to be integral member of your healthcare team. But the greatest improvements in health outcomes in the nineteenth century were the results of public hygiene and sanitation programs. You might not think about your utility company as a healthcare provider. However, electricity, clean water, heat, and even cell phone service are fundamental to living a healthy life in modern America. Utilities literally save lives by helping people make healthy, productive choices.

The WHO goes on to define health as "a state of complete physical, mental and social well-being and not merely the absence of disease."[2] When we think about a state of complete physical well-being, then health starts to include your primary care doctor, but also the park down the street where you exercise, the sports club, your grocery store, and even your car. When we talk about mental health, we are not just talking about depression, anxiety, addiction, and crazy people who end up dead or criminals, or both. Mental health includes managing daily stress, coping at work, dealing with grief, proper sleep, and wellness. Social well-being brings our core relationships—family and friends—into the discussion of health, as well. It also includes work relationships. It is hard to be healthy when you are poor, in debt, isolated from family, lonely, and unemployed. As you are quickly beginning to realize, being healthy is a community issue—not just an individual choice. When we focus on the process of health, we begin to see how health impacts every area of our life, and how every area—social, economic, environmental, genetic, and behavioral—is impacting the population health of a community.

# HEALTHCARE SYSTEMS SUCK AT PROMOTING HEALTH

Hospitals and clinics focus on illness, fail to promote health, and have little impact on the overall health outcomes in our communities. In the 1980s, David Kindig—godfather of population health—defined population health as the "the distribution of health outcomes within a population, the determinants that influence distribution, and the policies and interventions that affect the determinants." His definition is complete and insightful, but must be unpacked to be understandable. The first clause, "the distribution of health outcomes within a population," observes that at any given time in any particular community, some people are healthy and some people are sick. We can describe overall health of a population on a continuum of outcomes that are distributed across of range of healthy to sick. The second clause, "the determinants that influence distribution," notes that there are measurable drivers of health outcomes in communities. He goes on to break out the different determinants of health into several core domains: social, environmental, behavioral, genetic, and healthcare. The final clause, "and the policies and interventions that affect the determinants," alludes to a connection between the design of communities, especially the programs and policies that affect health, and health outcomes for similar individuals in different communities. It turns out that where you live and what you do impacts your health.

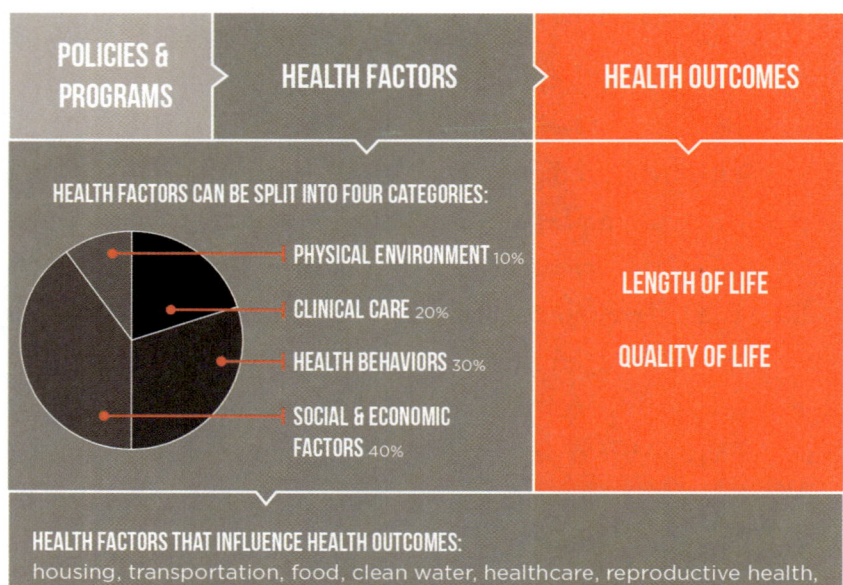

**FIGURE 2.1. Population Health Connects Policies and Programs to Health Factors to Community-Wide Health Outcomes.**

*There are many health factors that influence health outcomes: transportation, food, clean water, healthcare, reproductive health, behavioral health, exercise, tobacco, energy, jobs, child care, education, elder care, civic engagement and safety. Decades of research have quantified the impact of health factors on health outcomes. Clinical care—the services you receive from a hospital or clinic—accounts for about 20 percent (one-fifth) of health outcomes. For the majority of families, differences in behavior, social context, economic factors, and physical environment explain 80 percent (four-fifths) of community-wide health outcomes.*

┌ they cost the most though

The major insight was that healthcare—the hospitals, clinics, and medical services in a community—accounts for less than 20 percent, or one-fifth—of the observed variation in health outcomes. Or we might say, healthcare—as described by access to services and the quality of services your family receives—is much less important to

↳ where most of healthcare budget goes

the health of a community than we might expect. Health is primarily determined by who your parents are, where you live, what you do, and who you know. Healthcare systems—such as hospitals—might save your life if you get sick, but they are not set up to keep you healthy.

As a population health consultant working for an integrated health system in rural Wisconsin, I surveyed community leaders in business, social work, education, county health, healthcare, community foundations, and nonprofits. The central question was, "Why is our community health system broken?" I heard a number of complaints and concerns, but a few stood out because I heard them repeatedly. It didn't matter if folks worked in public health, social work, healthcare, or business, the pain points were similar for everyone:

- Privacy and legal concerns limit information-sharing between organizations.

- No sustainable funding stream for home-based or neighborhood-based services.

- Lack of capacity at key points in safety net (emergency housing, transportation to work/appointments, behavioral health access and navigation).

- Burdensome regulations—excessive rules and restrictions for families seeking to transform their lives.

- Distrust—a history of disappointment that goes both ways: community members distrust of interventions and organizations intended to help; community organizations have been burned by community members and distrust their clients.

- Systemic discrimination exists (including race, social-economic status, etc.) but we don't want to admit that it does; some folks need support that can be offered and do not take it, and some folks try to take more support than they need, leading to entitlement and dependence "on the system."

- Unhealthy competition between agencies, healthcare facilities, and community coalitions.

- No unified system to "know the data." Can't track clients between agencies; no triage system to address high-priority needs first.

If you consider the differing perspectives from which key players—healthcare systems, public health systems, social service systems, and local governments—view health, then the problems of fragmentation, duplication of efforts, and waste become obvious and consistent with competing systems that don't know how to collaborate.

Healthcare providers are trained to see disease through a bio-medical lens. When you are sick, a doctor thinks about the pathology and physiology of your symptoms, sends you to biochemical tests and anatomical images, and then diagnoses you based on biomedical explanations that lead to treatment recommendations that frequently include pharmaceutical drugs or surgery.

Public health has primarily been focused on prevention. The major advances in public health are in areas of preventing infections (vaccines and sanitation), safety (seatbelt, air bags, and sidewalks), behavioral health (smoking, alcohol, and drug use), and family planning. Public health takes a wider approach than healthcare, and it considers the social, economic, and environmental factors that lead to health or sickness. However, public health programs are frequently topic specific and underfunded. Public health is not as glamorous as medicine.

Social service providers—such as nonprofits, churches, and charities—have an important role to play in promoting health. In many communities, nonprofits, churches, and charities are often the "safety nets" that catches struggling families. These organizations include a wide variety of organizations (i.e., Catholic charities, Salvation Army, food pantries, and Big Brothers/Big Sisters). The organizations themselves are frequently small, independent, and staffed by motivated, caring individuals with a sense of purpose. Though most organizations may or may not have health improvement as a primary mission, the staff and volunteers are the frontline providers of services closely linked to population health outcomes. Because the factors that influence population health are not always profitable for business or affordable for the families who benefit most from the service, the government may act a central payer within the public health system, but will rely on an array of stakeholders to achieve its goals via grants and contracts. Insurance plans may pay for healthcare-related social expenses incurred by healthcare providers. Private philanthropy, foundations, and social investors typically seek to fund start-up or pilot programs expecting that program will eventual eventually achieve sustainability through free markets or government payments.

Payers have both political and economic viewpoints. Many programs are funded because they are population, even when the programs fail to improve community well-being. Some programs are funded because they are economically sensible, even when they are not politically expedient. There are many areas that would be politically popular and financially beneficial, but they lack a clear champion and vision for change that will mobilize funding to improve population health.

When we see how the different perspectives can lead to waste, delays, and frustrations for community members, then the need for reform becomes urgent and relevant to real struggles of workers and families.

## HAROLD BROKE HIS HIP—TRAPPED IN A SICK SYSTEM

There has been much written about healthcare super-users. One of my favorite essays was "Million Dollar Murray" by Malcolm Gladwell. The piece is more than a decade old, but it still resonates. Gladwell argues that it is easier and less expensive to solve a complex social problem—like homelessness—than it is to manage the medical consequences of unmet social needs. Gladwell concludes:

*Solutions [for complex social problems] have little appeal to the right, because they involve special treatment for people who do not deserve special treatment; and they have little appeal to the left, because their emphasis on efficiency over fairness suggests the cold number-crunching of Chicago-school cost-benefit analysis. Even the promise of millions of dollars in savings or cleaner air or better police departments cannot entirely compensate for such discomfort.*[3]

The debate about healthcare reform has renewed popular interest in our disaster-oriented healthcare system. Why disaster-oriented? A disaster-oriented system waits for people to break, then tries to fix the effects, instead of addressing the problem. T. R. Reid wrote an interesting think piece in *The Atlantic* in summer 2017. His essay, "How We Spend $3,400,000,000,000: Why More Than Half of America's Healthcare Spending Goes to Five Percent of Patients" highlights the reality than we spend one-sixth of our nations GDP, or more than $3.4 trillion, every year on healthcare. The number is huge, but it is not evenly distributed. A disproportionate amount of the spending is focused on a small number of very expensive patients:

> If that $3.4 trillion were spread equally throughout the population, the bill would come to some $10,350 for every man, woman, and child in the country. But fortunately—for most of us, anyway—the cost of healthcare is not equally distributed. Rather, a small number of Americans runs up most of the expense. The biggest medical costs are concentrated on a fairly small segment of the population—people with one or more chronic illnesses plus victims of accidents or violent crime. The cost is so concentrated that an estimated 5 percent of the population accounts for 50 percent of total medical costs.[4]

In attempt to make the true cost of health transparent to stakeholders in our community, I decided to shadow a super-user (a.k.a. platinum patient, a.k.a. frequent flier) through the healthcare system. In order to protect the patient's privacy, I will call him Harold. This is the story of how Harold broke his hip and was trapped in a sick system. I turned Harold's story into a cartoon and showed it to stakeholders through the community. His story is at once comic, tragic, and regrettable.

Harold lived alone in an apartment that was part of an assisted-living community. He qualified for Cash Assistance, Unemployment Insurance, Supplemental Security Income, and Housing Assistance. He had multiple case managers working through the county health department, social service agencies, and a local nonprofit. In some ways, the system was working: there were lots of systems funded by the safety net to protect Harold and provide for his needs. But

Harold was not a nice person, and he did not make good personal choices. He was mean to his caseworkers. He was an obese alcoholic with a mood disorder. I did not talk to anyone who liked working with Harold. One day, he fell in his apartment and broke his hip. It was two days before he was discovered by his caseworker, dirty, demented, and dying.

Harold was rushed to the hospital and admitted to the Orthopedic Surgery service, and then nothing happened. Harold refused treatment. He fought with nursing. He ordered massive amounts of food and demanded loads of prescription painkillers. He had a serious problem—a broken hip—complicated by a variety of issues, including poorly managed substance abuse, and personality and mental health issues.

Eventually, a multidisciplinary team was able to get Harold the medical help he needed. Yet the prolonged hospitalization and rehab led to Harold's eviction from his apartment. Now Harold was getting healthy, but he was homeless and refused to be discharged without a safe place to go. Case workers, social workers, county managers, social service agencies, lawyers, and nurses worked to find Harold a safe, affordable place to live in the community. A month passed, and finally the system found Harold an acceptable apartment. He was discharged. Less than a week later, he overdosed on his prescription medications and the police brought him back—kicking and screaming—to the emergency department.

Harold—when he was not drunk and consistently taking his behavior medications—could be a nice person. When he had transportation to clinic appointments and reminders to fill his prescriptions, then he could function in the community. However, there was no handoff between the healthcare system and the community services that had kept Harold out of the hospital before. In the absence of a clear community care plan and with Harold's history of being a jerk, he floundered and failed even after the healthcare system spent hundreds of thousands of dollars fixing his hip. To put this in context, Harold's one hospitalization that was directly related to his substance abuse issues cost the healthcare system more than the annual salary of a psychiatrist, social worker, and public health nurse—combined. It was not possible to address Harold's health issues without tackling the social and the medical problems together.

I discussed Harold's situation with case managers, frontline workers, first responders, telephone nurse advisors, hospital administrators, social workers, and high-risk care coordinators. We discussed the opportunities and barriers to helping someone like Harold. We talked for three hours, and we managed to troubleshoot only the first step in the process: getting Harold from the hospital to his apartment in a safe, timely, and human fashion. Harold's case was complex and highlighted the limitations of our fragmented system. There was confusion about who should be notified first. There were questions about how to protect Harold's privacy. Participants were torn between honoring the choices of a stubborn old man and intervening early to prevent a mentally ill individual from hurting himself. There were issues with information sharing, problems with pre-authorizations for preventative services, funding for rehabilitation treatments, durable medical treatments, and outpatient prescriptions. There *problems* were long wait times for community behavioral health providers. There were separate, incompatible electronic medical records that led to confusion between clinic and hospital providers. In the end, we settled on four learning points that might help super-users such as Harold in the future:

1.    Connect social factors and medical outcomes.

2.    Address social factors early and reassess frequently.

3. Coordinate between care coordination agencies.

4. Pay for community-based (as opposed to hospital-based) services.

For a practicing pediatrician accustomed to treating families, not just individuals, it was obvious we treat the whole person—not just the medical problem. For a trained public health expert, it makes sense to connect social factors to important health outcomes. But it takes a new set of tools and strategies to begin to systematically and specifically identify and address the social factors that drive over-utilization of healthcare services. In the case of Harold the Snowman, there was no financial incentive to keep him healthy. It turned out that it was expensive to solve Harold's social problems. However, the cost of treating Harold's medical needs was twenty times more than it would cost to solve Harold's social problems. *short time fix vs. long time fix*

Population health represents the local community-based efforts by frontline workers to address the upstream risk factors that are driving the major health outcomes for patients such as Harold. Your community will call the grassroots effort by a different name, but population health connects the innovative efforts by programs, agencies, and organizations across a community. The connection is based on a shared vision to address the upstream causes of health and disease, collaborate across disciplines, and ensure the best outcomes for families where they live, work, learn, play, and worship. There are many motivations for stakeholders to participate in improving population health. One common theme is summed up by the African proverb: "If you want to go fast, run alone. If you want to go far, run together." By collaborating, communities can go further and farther than ever before, and make a life-changing impact on vulnerable families and isolated seniors.

# CULTURE OF HEALTH PROVIDES A PATHWAY TO POPULATION HEALTH

| 10 PRINCIPLES TO IMPROVE POPULATION HEALTH OUTCOMES | |
|---|---|
| Good health flourishes across geographic, demographic, and social sectors. | Everyone has access to affordable, quality healthcare because it is essential to maintain, or reclaim, health. |
| Attaining the best health possible is valued by our entire society. | Healthcare is efficient and affordable. |
| Individuals and families have the means and opportunity to make choices that lead to the healthiest lives possible. | The economy is less burdened by excessive and unwarranted healthcare spending. |
| Business, government, individuals, and organizations work together to build healthy communities. | Keeping everyone as healthy as possible guides public and private decision making. |
| No one is excluded. | Americans understand that we are all in this together. |
| www.cultureofhealth.org | |

**TABLE 2.2. 10 Principles to Improve Population Health Outcomes**

*The Robert Wood Johnson Foundation has launched a major policy initiative, "Culture of Health." The goal of a culture of health is for communities to work together to replicate scalable solutions and take targeted actions to improve the health and well-being of all people. There are ten key principles that can help your community build a culture of health that will transform programs and policies and accelerate the transition toward better population health outcomes at scale. You can learn more about building a culture of health at: www.cultureofhealth.org.*

For decades, the Robert Wood Johnson Foundation (RWJF) has been a thought leader and philanthropic powerhouse behind innovations in population health. RJWF advocates for a Culture of Health approach to systems change. If we want to improve the health and well-being of a population, then we must focus on the actionable and primary drivers that can improve health.

We know that change is coming to both the US healthcare system and the US safety net. We are spending more every year, yet still failing to protect families. It is inevitable; change is coming. In the next decade, we will see the safety net, including Medicaid, completely restructured. Federal funding will be cut; state budgets will be stretched thin. This represents the defining challenge (and critical opportunity) for county health departments to partner with businesses, nonprofits, churches, social service organizations, and healthcare systems to address the social determinants of health that drive health outcomes.

A culture of health is the opposite of the disaster-oriented healthcare that we are continually providing to our most vulnerable community members. It is an alternative to the status quo and an opportunity to improve the health and well-being of everyone in our community.

## LEADERS WHO MODELED A CULTURE OF HEALTH FOR ME

A Culture of Health was taught to me by a number of teachers and mentors. I have been blessed to learn a number of amazing, thoughtful leaders, as shown here.

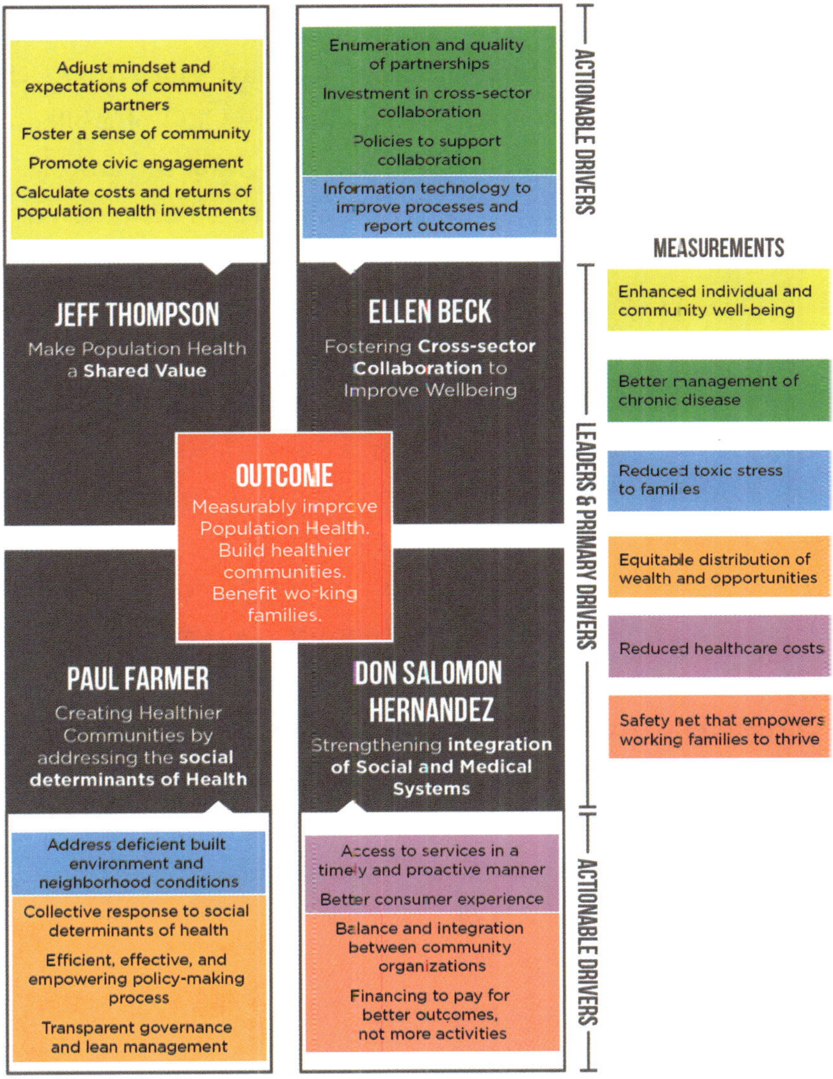

## ACTIONABLE DRIVERS

**Adjust mindset and expectations of community partners**

Foster a sense of community

Promote civic engagement

Calculate costs and returns of population health investments

---

Enumeration and quality of partnerships

Investment in cross-sector collaboration

Policies to support collaboration

Information technology to improve processes and report outcomes

## LEADERS & PRIMARY DRIVERS

### JEFF THOMPSON
Make Population Health a **Shared Value**

### ELLEN BECK
Fostering **Cross-sector Collaboration** to Improve Wellbeing

### OUTCOME
Measurably improve Population Health. Build healthier communities. Benefit working families.

### PAUL FARMER
Creating Healthier Communities by addressing the **social determinants of Health**

### DON SALOMON HERNANDEZ
Strengthening **integration of Social and Medical Systems**

## ACTIONABLE DRIVERS

Address deficient built environment and neighborhood conditions

Collective response to social determinants of health

Efficient, effective, and empowering policy-making process

Transparent governance and lean management

---

Access to services in a timely and proactive manner

Better consumer experience

Balance and integration between community organizations

Financing to pay for better outcomes, not more activities

## MEASUREMENTS

Enhanced individual and community well-being

Better management of chronic disease

Reduced toxic stress to families

Equitable distribution of wealth and opportunities

Reduced healthcare costs

Safety net that empowers working families to thrive

---

## TABLE 2.3. Leaders Who Taught Me about a Culture of Health

*It is one thing to read about a culture of health; it is another to see it lived out in a community. There have been four dynamic leaders who lived out a culture of health and modeled for me how communities can be transformed. The key for me was to learn from men and women working in different sectors (business, nonprofit, university, and church), while remembering that every sector can and should participate in a culture of health.*

## 1. Shared Values—Jeff Thompson

I have learned about the importance of shared values from Jeff Thompson. Jeff was the dynamic and visionary CEO of a billion-dollar integrated healthcare system. He is thoughtful and articulate, and a master at motivating people. He also started his career as a pediatrician. He has been a great mentor and inspiration for me. (Full disclosure: Jeff is also my father-in-law and I am so thankful to be married to his even-more-amazing daughter, Rachel.)

Jeff recently published a book, *Lead True* (2017), that masterfully compiled stories from the business, healthcare, and education fields, illustrating how a diverse group of leaders has employed value-based leadership and succeeded. These case studies offer dynamic, living narratives that demonstrate ways in which a leader, fueled by personal values, can change people, organizations, and even entire industries. In his book, there is a revealing anecdote. Jeff invites his readers to put themselves in place of a parent caring for a teenager debilitated by mental illness, potentially suicidal, and unsafe at home:

> *You are scared and unsure of what to do ... And the medical staff says that the hospital cannot admit your daughter, that it has no beds available in the psychiatric unit ... You are told, "Sorry, good luck. We can't help you." This [our nation's mental health crisis] is so hard for families, so hard on hospitals, but his is the kind of struggle that defines [healthcare] organizations. All of us have been touched by behavioral health or psychiatric problems, whether through our friends, coworkers, or our own families. Imagine that you are the leader of a healthcare organization or of your community's behavioral health department. What is your responsibility to that child, her family, and your community?*[5]

As the leader of an integrated health system, Jeff used this story as a way to motivate the organization to expand behavioral health services, build additional inpatient psychiatric beds, and partner with community agencies to improve access to services. The health system ultimately spent several million dollars to implement a model of focused-care coordinators that *decreased* hospital revenue by tens of millions of dollars. Why? Jeff though it was important to keep patients healthier and help them live fuller lives in the community, not in the hospital. The program spent more than $2 million a year on staff expenses that saved the community tens of millions of dollars by preventing illness, surgeries, and return hospitalizations that would have otherwise not been needed. "The best way for an organization to motivate a community," he says, "is to live a motivated life among them." Jeff strongly believes that great organizations live their values despite inconvenience of cost—they find a way. The commitment to values above profit and willingness to build shared need in the community made Jeff successful.

If we are going to collaborate to make population health a shared value, then we must speak clearly about what population health is, and articulate the shared value in language that is accessible and attractive to community partners. It will take time, effort, and patience to adjust the mindset and expectations of organizations that previously did not recognize their role in fostering a culture of health. But with time, persistence, kindness, and an accumulation of success, organizations in different sectors—healthcare, criminal justice, education, public health, social service, business, and nonprofits—will develop a sense of community. This community can lead to civic engagement, greater collaboration, shared resources, and systems change. With the right early decision about infrastructure and information technology, we will be able to calculate the cost and benefits of population health investments.

Population health will move from being a charitable project to a competitive advantage that allows neighborhoods, towns, and counties to attract high-paying jobs, retain talented employees, and launch successful businesses. The shared value will be grasped by all sectors of the community, but the benefits will accrue most directly to working families seeking a health place for their children to live, to learn, and to grow up healthy.

## 2. Collaboration—Ellen Beck

In communities where competition is the norm, collaboration can seem abnormal. One strategy other communities have used with success is to begin by enumerating instances where cross-sector coordination, cooperation, or integration led to systems change.

In medical school, I worked at the student-run free clinic founded by Ellen Beck. My earliest clinical experiences were in a profoundly collaborative, community-based system that empowered individuals to help each other. The UCSD Student-Run Free Clinic Project, in partnership with the community, provides accessible, quality healthcare for the underserved in a respectful environment in which students, health professionals, patients, and community members learn from one another. Beck was a master of "social Tai Chi." Social Tai Chi is not an official discipline, but rather the ability to move smoothly and calmly, redirecting institutional resistance toward positive social ends. In other contexts, this is known as "emotional intelligence." But if you have ever worked with Beck, social tai chi describes her approach perfectly. First, the free clinics are located at elementary schools, churches, and community buildings. Mobile clinics go to streets at night to address the chronic care needs of the homeless community, and go out the field to provide occupa-tional health services to migrant workers. At clinics, there are physi-cians, physicians in training, retired physicians, pharmacist, dentists, ophthalmologist, masseuse, psychiatrists, and health specialists. The clinics focus on hard-to-manage chronic conditions—diabetes, hypertension, dyslipidemia, depression, and anxiety—in hard-to-reach populations. But the true genius of Beck is the way she uses the free clinic to influence medical students.

Typically, medical students embark on their training with empathy, compassion, and a desire to make a difference. However, several studies provide evidence that their attitudes toward the underserved and empathy decline as students progress through their medical training. When undergraduate applicants are interview-ing for coveted positions at the medical school, they tell stories of volunteering oversees and serving the poor, and say things like, "I just love helping people." By the end of the third year of medical school, the same students take the ROAD to success: Radiology, Orthopedic Surgery, Anesthesiology, and Dermatology. They are tired of difficult patients with bad habits and unsolvable social situ-ations. The passion for primary care has been replaced by a desire for prestige, financial rewards, and comfortable lifestyles. Beck col-laborated with the community to create the free clinics, and then began to influence students to pursue careers in primary care. She recognizes the important part of medical education that occurs as a socialization and enculturation process, where students learn a set of customs and values through their daily experiences that reflect values of the profession of medicine, without being taught.

Not everyone needs to start a community free clinic. But even if the initiative is not focused on health, it is useful to build on histori-cal success and identify local champions capable of working across boundaries and barriers. As the partnerships and coordinated efforts multiply, it will be helpful to consider the quality of collaboration. Leaders will be able to forge deeper, stronger bonds with more diverse partners. Initiatives will be able to work at greater economies of scale. Beck taught me to use social tai chi to effect institutional change. I try to use resistance to my advantage. Risk of new endeavors will be spread across multiple organizations. Collaboration—in the right setting—will become a prerequisite for new programs. As an added benefit, successful collaborations frequently lead to new investment in cross-sector initiatives, policies to support future collaboration, and openness to information technology to improve processes and report outcomes. Over time, systems will change to make population health a priority in all policies and programs, and collaboration the default strategy for improving population health.

## 3. Social Determinants of Health—Paul Farmer

For my masters in public health, I wanted to learn from experts with real-world experience in population health. My goal was to soak up knowledge from physicians who had engaged deeply and meaningfully with communities to transform systems, improve service delivery, and address the root causes of disease. Medical anthropologist and physician Paul Farmer has dedicated his life to improving healthcare for the world's poorest people. He is a founding director of Partners In Health (PIH), an international nonprofit organization that since 1987 has provided direct healthcare services for families who are sick and living in poverty. Farmer began his lifelong commitment to Haiti in 1983 while still a student, working with dispossessed farmers in Haiti's Central Plateau. For three decades, Farmer has led colleagues working in twelve sites throughout Haiti and twelve additional countries around the globe. The work has become a model of healthcare for poor communities worldwide, and provides the basis for a science of health delivery.

Farmer organizes a Global Health Delivery (GHD) course at Harvard School of Public Health. It was created as a joint project between the School of Public Health, School of Business, and Medical School; [the goal was to bridge the gap between aspirations and action.] Using thirty case studies, GHD teaches how to deliver better care at lower costs. I took the course to learn how to create better value for communities through improved healthcare delivery, building on insights popularized by Michael Porter in *Redefining Health Care* (2006), which imagines a health system focused on the *value* of healthcare: *maximum social benefit per dollar spent*. It was clear that health delivery should emphasize *value*, as opposed to the traditional focus on volume, access, and equity of services. GHD has instructed thousands of students, ranging from doctors to law students to national health directors, in value-based health delivery that addresses the social determinants of health.

## 4. Connecting Social Factors to Medical Outcomes—Don Salomon Hernandez

Even before I went to medical school, I learned about how transformative connecting social and medical systems can be. An evangelical missionary to Central America introduced me to Don Salomon Hernandez. Don Salomon started as a rural pastor working in the mountains of Guatemala to support Quiché Mayan communities. He and his family endured a thirty-year civil war, natural disasters, and unimaginable hardship. In 1976, a major earthquake hit central Guatemala, leveling villages and killing nearly twenty-three thousand people and wounding an additional seventy-seven thousand in one day. The adobe brick buildings of Salomon's hometown, Uspantán, were flattened. Without electricity, running water, or road access to the capital, the village was cut off from help for months. US churches heard about Don Salomon's town and arranged to transfer cash to Guatemala. Missionaries transported the cash from the capital city to Uspantán by a combination of truck and mule. The money was intended to rebuild Salomon's home and small church. However, Don Salomon had a different idea: he bought a kiln and started making bricks.

Over the next year, Don Salomon's bricks would rebuild the town, the schools, the post office, roads, and more than a hundred homes. After the town was rebuilt, Don Salomon built a clinic, and multiple schoolhouses in the surrounding villages.

As a college student, I began organizing teams of volunteers—dentists, agronomists, and bankers—to travel to Guatemala, partner with the Hernandez family, and scale-up the vision of this amazing man. One of our first projects was a schoolhouse in the village where Rigoberta Menchú—world-famous author and 1992 Nobel Peace Prize winner—was born. Menchú won the Nobel Prize "in recognition of her work for social justice . . . for indigenous peoples." She is an amazing woman with a proud legacy of international reform. However, her reputation in her hometown was mixed. For a variety of political and social reasons, she had not returned home after the end of the civil war and the work of her companies, Salud Para Todos (Health for All) and Farmacias Simalares, to offer low-cost pharmaceuticals to indigenous communities in Central America had not reached her hometown.

At first, the plan was build an outreach clinic that would allow Quiché families to access preventative health services. However, when the plan was presented to the community elders, it was rejected. Yes, the community needed healthcare, but they also needed a schoolhouse. The priority was education, not immuniza-tions. The community was willing to purchase the land, contract with a local construction company, build with Don Salomon's bricks, and construct a schoolhouse. International volunteers supplied the funding and labor, but also connected with Guatemalan civic rights attorneys to advocate for federal financial aid to pay the salaries of a village teacher. Ultimately, we were able to build a schoolhouse, sustain it with public money, and create an outreach clinic to connect the village with preventative health serves. This was the first of many trips over three years for me. I would continue to travel to Guatemala, even during medical school, and learn from Don Salomon how to address social needs while improving access to medical care. He was a genius at accomplishing multiple things at once.

A previous generation of medical leaders—such as Jeff Thompson, Ellen Beck, Paul Farmer, and Don Salomon Hernandez—influenced, inspired, trained, and empowered younger leaders to take action, to invest deeply in meaningful work close to home, and to embrace the potential for personal, systemic change. Boundary-crossing projects that engage the root causes of poor health, disease, and poverty. Advocates for systems recognize that patients with complex medical problems also have complex and unmet social needs. These patients seek relief downstream—in hospitals—for what are fundamentally upstream, community-based problems. Rishi Manchanda, MD MPH, co-founded HealthBegins, a network for healthcare profes-sionals interested in addressing the social determinants of health. In his work, Manchanda coined the term *Upstreamist* to describe "healthcare professionals who are equipped to transform the social and environmental conditions that make people sick."[6] He believes in the transformative power of clinicians committed to social justice and rooted in the community. No project for an Upstreamist would be adequately described as: healthcare, education, economic, informatics, public health, or community development. Upstreamist projects cross professional divisions and disciplines. My mentors were all Upstreamists who lived, worked, and loved the intersections between disciplines. Despite working in the in-between spaces, each mentor committed to build up a Culture of Health in their communities.

With an end goal of creating a Culture of Health, cities and counties will address population health through shared visions, collaboration, social determinants of health, and integrated social and medical systems. These efforts will not be viewed as charity. Rather, key stakeholders will collaborate because better living and working conditions will reduce healthcare costs, build the local tax base, support local business, and attract talented workers. Plus, the work of population health, especially the process of making the health consequences of policy decisions explicit, obvious, and easy to understand will support collective response on social issues. Sewing up the safety net will not be viewed as merely a diversity issue or a poverty issue or a government issue; sewing up the safety net will be a personal issue. People will see the ways that population health promotes equity, improves health for everyone, and benefits working families, poor families, and successful families.

↳improves quality of life

## PRAIRIE DOG APPROACH FOR BETTER HEALTH

Prairie dogs are a fantastic example of an Upstreamist's mentality. Prairie dogs are communal animals. These cute cousins of the ground squirrel thrive in the grasslands of North America. They have adapted to live in areas prone to environmental threats, like hailstorms, blizzards, floods, and droughts, by digging highly complex and inter-connected burrows called "towns." A prairie dog town may contain as many as twenty-five family groups. The tunnels facilitate face-to-face connections.

Most importantly, these subsurface thoroughfares allow for protection from predators. Above ground, a lone prairie dog would be a tasty snack for a fox, hawk, weasel, and coyote. Their grassland home is literally swarming with apex predators ready to pounce on an unsuspecting and exposed rodent. Prairie dogs have developed a highly advance warning system that varies according to the source of danger. When one prairie dog spots a potential threat, she barks loudly.

Population health wants to help frontline workers act more like prairies dogs. We need caring individuals to form relationships across organizations. Our towns need easy-to-use thoroughfares between service agencies. We also need shared alert systems for when families are at risk. But we also need to recognize that the social services in America are both under-funded and under-attack. Leaders from government, healthcare systems, business, academics, and nonprofits frequently act like apex predators instead of partners. They pounce on innovators. They stalk new sources of revenue. And they compete for scarce resources, often hoarding information, funding, and expertise. But we cannot blame leaders for their predatory behavior. They have been trained and rewarded by a broken social service sector that incentivized individual success and an academic system that prizes originality over reproducibility. Thus, frontline workers who seek to collaborate have been driven underground.

*Underground*, as a noun, refers to "a group or movement organized secretly to work against an existing regime." For instance, the protagonist from a World War II spy novel might whisper, "I got involved with the French Underground." Or you have heard of the Underground Railroad, the network of secret routes and safe houses used by nineteenth-century slaves in the United States in efforts to escape to free states and Canada with the aid of abolitionists and allies who were sympathetic to their cause. This clandestine, informal operation was instrumental in the emancipation of thousands of black Southern slaves.

It is important to recognize that when frontline workers organize, collaborate, and cooperate, this can be a subversive act. People in power may be (and should be) afraid of the transformative energy released when good people get together for the right reasons. The idea of a Population Health Underground taps into the rich history of social rebellions, encapsulates the groundbreaking work of individuals collaborating in communities across the US, and pins a label on a number of different social upswellings in towns just like yours.

## BE WARY OF IMPROBABLE EXPECTATIONS

We should be careful about putting too much emphasis on succeeding against adversity. Base rate is a statistical concept that looks at predictors of outcomes we are interested in—good or bad—as they are influenced by how frequently the outcome occurs in the general population. In the radio series *Busted: America's Poverty Myths*, the host, Brooke Gladstone, warns that we should "beware of unicorns."[7] There is no shortage of news coverage of rags-to-riches stories, self-made millionaires, and entrepreneurs who pulled themselves up by their bootstraps. There will always be a miracle child who survives or a catastrophic accident that kills. The problem is that when you look at only the exceptional stories, it is easy to conclude that the factors separating rich from poor, or healthy from sick, are the All-American values: hard work, discipline, and self-control. The concept of base rates—and by extension, risk—illustrates how success (and

→ it's by chance – connections experiences environment

failure) is conditioned by the social context where we live, work, learn, play, and age. Talent and hard work matter; I am not denying self-determination. But we must distinguish between the luck of individuals and the system factors contributing to health and disease.

└→ why we look at statistics, not individual cases

## HEALTH EQUITY AS EXPLAINED BY UNICORNS

Picture three unicorns caught in a flood. It is possible that with enough effort, all three might be able to survive until they are rescued. However, the unicorns are not all the same height. In a free-for-all no-help-for-anyone scenario, tall unicorns have an advantage—it takes no extra effort or talent to keep his head above water. In this case, height is a risk factor that predicts the likelihood of success (tall unicorns survive) or failure (short unicorns drown).

## FREE-FOR-ALL

## EQUAL

## EQUITABLE

 **FIGURE 2.3 Unicorns Explain Health Equity**

*There are three strategies for improving health equity. A free-for-all approach doesn't provide aid during a crisis; every unicorn is left to sink-or-swim based on their own skill, talents, and resources. A fair system gives each unicorn the same aid regardless of*

*his or her needs. Finally, a smart and equitable approach focuses on the outcome—surviving the flood—and allocates resources so that every unicorn survives. Health equity means everyone has an opportunity to thrive. It acknowledges that it's harder for little unicorns to survive. We can make an effort to improve health for everyone—especially little unicorns that face the biggest obstacles.*

A *fair or equal system* will provide the same interventions to everyone, regardless of their risk. In our unicorn analogy, a *fair system* might give every unicorn one box to stand on. No one gets special treatment; everyone is treated equally. However, a fair or equal system that distributes extra help to everyone equally is wasted on the tallest unicorn, helps the average unicorn, and is wasted on the smallest unicorn. In many ways, *a fair system is the most wasteful.* You have invested three boxes of stuff—but only helped one unicorn achieve success (one achieved on its own, and the other still drowned). A *smart system*—as opposed to a fair system—will align investments with opportunities to change outcomes. In the last example, the tallest unicorn gets no box, the average unicorn gets one box, and the shortest unicorn gets two boxes. *This is not a fair arrangement. However, it is the strategy that is equitable and effective.* The smart plan—which considers risk as criteria for distributing resources—makes targeted investments in order to give everyone the best opportunity to achieve success.

When we think about reforming the safety net, we are often thinking about the upstream policy and design choices made by our national and local leaders. However, the downstream effects on our families, our neighborhoods, and our cities go examined. Rather than focusing on the shortfall of safety net programs that are federally controlled, we should prioritize the programs that have greatest local variation and use the decentralized safety net to improve our communities. Programs with significant state discretion include child support, unemployment insurance, target employment, cash assistance, childcare subsides, early education, and state taxes. We have the most local control over early child development, income, employment, housing, and child healthcare. These are areas where we can match federal funding to local programs.

There is significant variability in the amount of local discretion in how the safety net is financed, administered, and implemented. The Institute for Research on Poverty, University of Wisconsin-Madison published a very interesting analysis on the safety net entitled *Separate and Unequal: The Dimensions and Consequences of Safety Net Decentralization in the US 1994–2014*. Researchers Sarah Bruch, Marcia Meyers, and Janet Gornick considered the benefits for eleven federal–state programs that constitute the core of safety net provision for working-age adults and families: cash assistance, food assistance, health insurance, child support, child care, preschool/early education, unemployment insurance, state income taxes, cash assistance work assistance, disability assistance, and housing assistance. They examined the extent of cross-state inequality in social provision and found substantial variation across states, variation that is consistent with policy design differences in state discretion.

Rather than focusing on the shortfall of safety net programs that are federally controlled, we should prioritize the programs that have greatest local variation and use the decentralized safety net to improve our communities. Programs with significant state discretion include: child support, unemployment insurance, targeted employment, cash assistance, childcare subsides, early education, and state taxes. We have the most local control over early child development, income, employment, housing and child healthcare.[8] These are areas where we can match federal funding to local programs.

There is significant political energy addressing the challenges facing healthcare at the national level. But I think that the real opportunity for meaningful progress is at the local level. It will be frontline workers who coordinate and collaborate to make local institutions benefit working families.

No longer is it acceptable for social services to be fragmented, duplicative, wasteful, inefficient, unsustainable, and marginalized; you know, *dumb*. There is a grassroots movement powered by like-minded service providers who are working to overturn the status quo. We want *smart* programs targeted at local needs that prioritize families who will benefit from services. Communities and community members alike are demanding that population health programs address social risk factors—such as housing, transportation, unemployment, violence, addiction, poverty, and education—while improving health outcomes for everyone, regardless of race, gender, age, ethnicity, sexual orientation, religion, or political party. Population health resources already exist in your hometown: the challenge is to find them, mark them, and point families to them.

## REFLECTION QUESTIONS

1.  How can healthcare systems and county health departments help nonprofits in their efforts to tackle social problems?

2.  What are three basic social trends that effect health in your community? What would it take to accelerate positive changes toward improved population health?

3.  Think about Ellen Beck and her social Tai Chi. What are the ways that you can turn bureaucratic resistance to change into an asset? Can you redirect strengths to achieve better population health? Can you do something subtle

that addresses the rapid social, technological, or economic changes buffeting your community?

4.   Where in your community do Population Health Prairie Dogs congregate? Is there a coffee shop, bar, breakfast joint, or club that would be a friendly neutral space to connect across organizations?

5.   Who are your local political leaders? How might you influence city and county government to help sew up the safety net and benefit working families?

---

## PART 2 ENDNOTES

1   Michael Marmot, "Health in an Unequal World," *Harveian Oration* presented by Royal College of Physicians, London, UK, on Oct 18, 2006.
2   Health. http://www.who.int/about/mission/en/
3   Malcolm Gladwell, "Million Dollar Murray," *Gladwell.com* (Feb. 2006), http://gladwell.com/million-dollar-murray/
4   T. R. Reid. "How We Spend $3,400,000,000,000," *The Atlantic* (June 2017), www.theatlantic.com/health/archive/2017/06/how-we-spend-3400000000000/530355/
5   Jeff Thompson, *Lead True: Live Your Values, Build Your People, Inspire Your Community* (Charleston, SC: Forbes Press, 2016).
6   Rishi Manchanda, "What Is an Upstreamist in Healthcare?" *Institute for Healthcare Improvement* (2015), www.ihi.org/Documents/OpenSchoolCourseTranscripts/RishiUpstreamist.htm
7   Brooke Gladstone, "Busted: America's Poverty Myths." *On the Media.* WNYC Studios (2016), www.wnyc.org/series/busted-americas-poverty-myths
8   Sarah K. Bruch, Marcia K. Meyers, and Janet C. Gornick, "Separate And Unequal: The Dimensions And Consequences of Safety Net Decentralization in the U.S. 1994–2014," *Instittue for Research on Poverty* (2016), http://inequality.stanford.edu/publications/media/details/dimensions-and-consequences-safety-net-decentralization

# THE SIMPSONS EXPLAIN THE SOCIAL DETERMINANTS OF HEALTH

**CHALLENGE:** Can a fictional family—the Simpsons—explain the social determinants of health in a way that redefines the way we view healthy communities?

Social determinants of health (SDH) are "the structural determinants and conditions in which people are born, grow, live, work and age." They include factors like socioeconomic status, education, the physical environment, employment, and social support networks, as well as access to healthcare.

We often overlook the impact of the SDH because they are common, ubiquitous, "normal," and, therefore, invisible. But the SDH are a matter of life and death. They affect the way people live, their consequent chance of illness, and their risk of premature death.

We watch in wonder as life expectancy and good health continue to increase in some counties across the US, and in alarm as others fail to improve or get worse.

These inequities in health—preventable, avoidable, and fixable—arise because of the circumstances where families grow, live, work, and age. There are systems in place to help families prosper and thrive, like healthcare systems, public health systems, social services, education systems, local government, and legal systems. Thus, political, social, and economic forces shape the conditions that affect families.

Social and economic policies at a federal, state, county, and city level have a determining impact on whether a child can grow and develop to her full potential and live a flourishing life, or whether her life will be blighted with turmoil, illness, and an untimely death. I believe that the development of a society, rich or poor, can be judged by the quality of its population's health, how justly health is distributed across the social spectrum, and the degree of protection provided from disadvantages as a result of ill health.

## WHY SHOULD FAMILIES BE CONCERNED ABOUT SDH?

We cannot address population health without first focusing on the SDH. An unhealthy community tends to cause poverty, and poverty leads to poor health. Individual families do not have the resources to pay for all the prerequisites of good health, but they do bear the burden of unhealthy environments through unsafe housing, lost wages, out-of-pocket healthcare costs, poor schools, and food deserts.

David Bloom, a professor at Harvard School of Public Health, was the chair of the Population Health department while I was doing my MPH. He taught Population Health 101. He would frequently reference research that a healthy population spurs economic growth. He notes:

> *First, healthier people are more economically productive. Better health also leads to an increase in savings rates— because healthier people expect to live longer and are naturally more concerned with their future financial needs.*
>
> *Unhealthy children may enter school with physical and cognitive disadvantages, miss more days of school, attend school for fewer years, and learn less when they're in school. By contrast, healthy children are more likely to be able to take advantage of whatever education is available to them— and a good education has profound economic consequences throughout an individual's life. These consequences include a higher starting wage and larger salary increases over the course of one's working life—earnings that ripple out into the larger economy.*[1]

A healthy community provides better jobs for working parents and better schools for their children. Working families care about population health because it impacts them where they live, where they work, and where their children learn.

Families care about the population because population health affects their children. If you look at what drives voters every election, the top issues are usually: economy, jobs, education, healthcare, and safety. The social determinants of health gives families a tool to evaluate the success (or failure) of the community to deliver on the American Dream—a house, a job, a healthy family, and children who opportunities to grow up and be successful. Working parents care about whether or not they live in a good school district, whether it is safe or not for their daughter to ride her bike and their son to play in the park. Families want to know if their baby is at risk of lead poisoning due to bad housing, or poisoned tap water. It is also important that their children are able to graduate high school, avoid trouble (including gangs, drug, and unsafe sex), and be able to either go to college or get a well-paying job. All of these aspirations are captured in the concept of social determinants of health.

## THE TYPICAL AMERICAN FAMILY LIVES IN SPRINGFIELD

The Simpsons, the cartoon family, are an archetypical middle class, white, working family. Homer is the primary source of income for the family and makes about $11.99 per hour or $37,416 per year as a nuclear safety inspector—specifically, the pusher of the red button—at the local power plant, a monotonous task at risk of replacement due to machine automation in the real world.[2]

Homer has all the trappings of a stereotypical working-class American: He lives in a modest home in the suburbs with his wife and three children. He works at a factory job while his wife Marge tends to the children and cooks. He is not a college graduate. He drinks beer, loves to grill, and wears a white polo shirt and blue jeans. Based on income, wealth, consumption, demographics, or aspirations, the Simpsons are middle-class Americans.

Equally important, Homer, Marge, Bart, Lisa, and Maggie live in Springfield, a unique city in that it is both fictitious and conveniently located in whatever state will best serve the needs of a particular episode.

There has been significant argument over where the real Springfield is. Matt Groening—the Simpson's creator—likes the debate. He said, "Springfield was one of the most common names for a city in the US. . . . I thought, 'This will be cool; everyone will think it's their Springfield.'" However, the location of Springfield dramatically effects whether or not the Simpson's family will struggle or thrive. The Simpsons are an average family and earn an average household income in a majority of Springfields. It is helpful to use them as a benchmark to compare how regional variations in health factors effect population health.

Median household incomes vary by location. In some areas, the job market is strong; in others, families struggle to survive. We can look at how Homer's income compares to the median income in all the US counties with a town called "Springfield."

In addition, a large portion of the wealth of a middle-class family is derived from home ownership. The Simpsons have lived in their home, 742 Evergreen Terrace, for more than twenty years. At this point, we can assume that they—like most middle-class families who take out thirty-year mortgages—have significant equity built up, but also monthly mortgage payments.

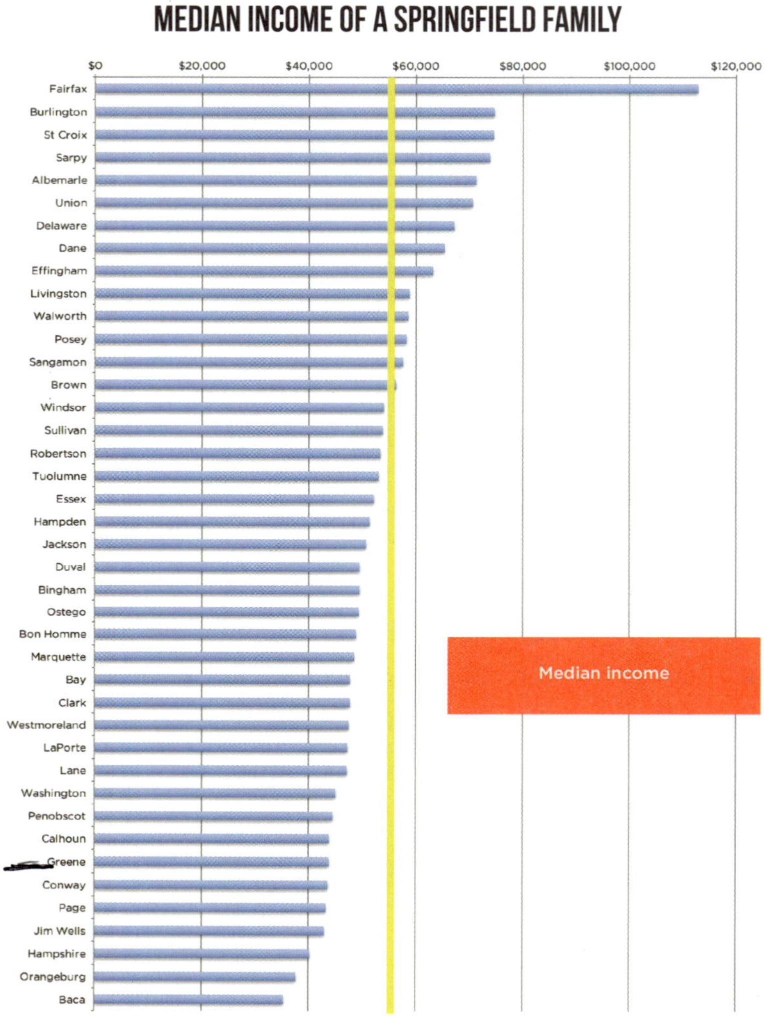

## MEDIAN INCOME OF A SPRINGFIELD FAMILY

**FIGURE 3.1. Median Income of a Springfield Family**

*Income can come from jobs, investments, government assistance programs, or retire-ment plans. Income allows families and individuals to purchase health insurance and medical care but also provides options for healthy lifestyle choices. Homer's job at the power plant results in an above-average income in more than half of the Springfields. However, the range wide of median incomes, from less than $40,000 to more than $110,000, highlights the importance of local factors on economic opportunities. Source: www.countyhealthrankings.org*

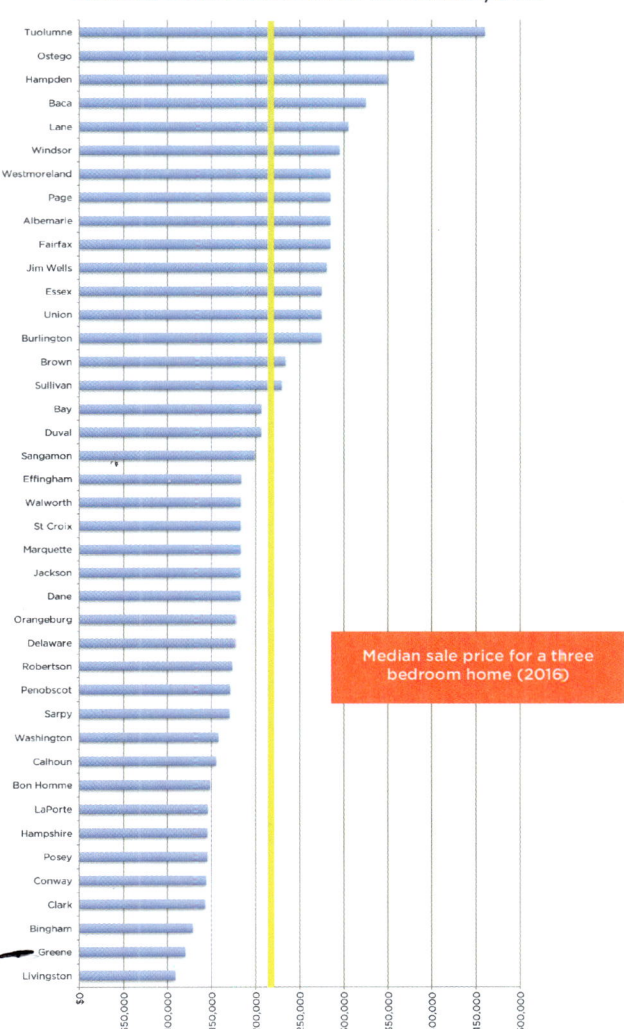

# MEDIAN HOME VALUE IN SPRINGFIELD, USA

Median sale price for a three bedroom home (2016)

**FIGURE 3.2. Median Home Value in Springfield, USA**

*Home ownership has been the foundation of the medical class dream for the majority of the twentieth century. Homeowners increase wealth over time, add equity every month, get mortgage tax deductions, establish credit, and help families save money. However, social and economic trends are making home ownership more difficult. Depending on which Springfield you may live, the cost of home ownership may vary by as much as $300,000! Source: https://www.trulia.com/home_prices/*

Even though the Simpsons have a steady income and own their home, there is not money left in the monthly budget to pay for health. This means that the community where they live has a huge impact on their well-being. These community factors—the social determinants of health—are influenced by a variety of cultural, economic, political, and environmental forces. When we talk about the social determinants of health, we are referring to [conditions that allow families to thrive as well as the obstacles beyond an individual's control that prevent families from experiencing health.] The WHO defines health as a "a state of complete physical, mental, and social well-being and not merely the absence of disease or infirmity." However, the connections between the social determinants and health outcomes are not always obvious.

Even though the connection is not obvious, we can see clear differences in life expectancy across communities. Years of potential life lost (YPLL) is a measure of premature mortality that is standardized to a community of a hundred thousand. Premature deaths are deaths that occur before a person reaches an expected age (e.g. age seventy-five). Many of these deaths are considered to be preventable.

# PREMATURE DEATH BY COUNTY — SPRINGFIELD MAY BE KILLING YOU

## Years of Potential Life Lost (YPLL) per 100,000

YPLL = the difference between normal life expectancy (75 years) and age of death for people living in the county

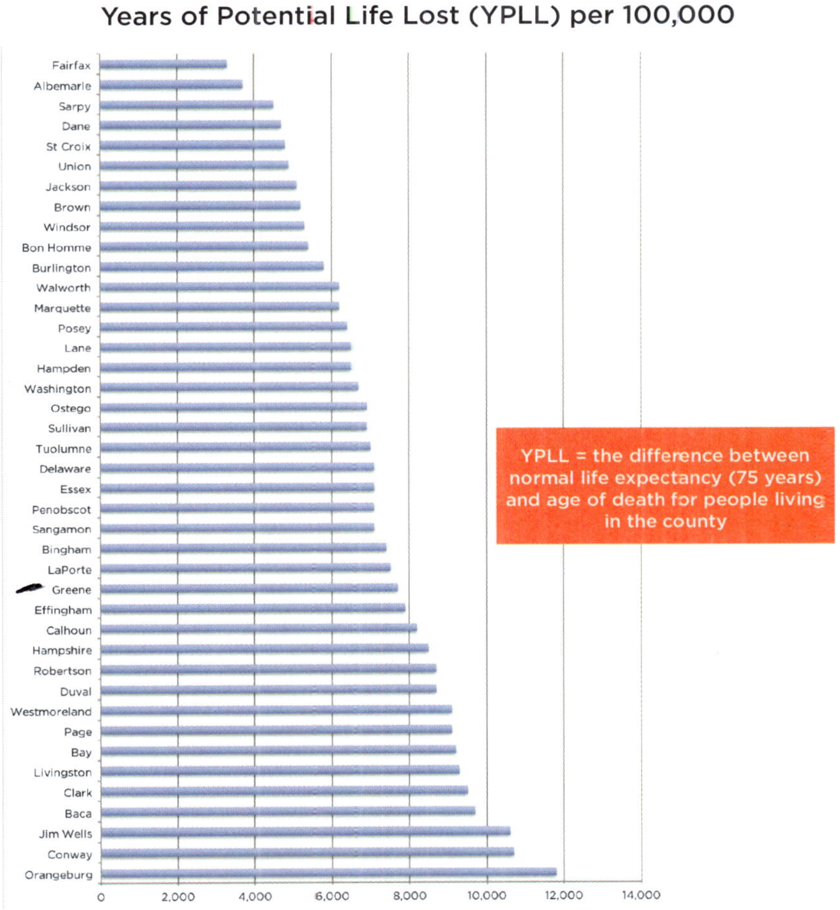

**FIGURE 3.3. Premature Death by County—Springfield May Be Killing You**

*Most people expect that premature deaths may be more common for families living in resource-starved villages in Africa or war-torn Middle Eastern cities. However, healthy communities gain more than eight thousand years of life per a hundred thousand. YPLL emphasizes the processes underlying premature mortality in a population. Many people are shocked to see the regional variation across US counties can approach the same variation we observe between developed and developing nations. Source: www.county-healthrankings.org*

## HOW DOES SPRINGFIELD MEASURE UP?

In 2017, County Health Rankings & Roadmaps released the newest set of county-level measures pulled from a variety of national data sources intended to illustrate what we know when it comes to keeping people healthy or making people sick and how the opportunity for good health differs from one county to the next. For Homer, Marge, Bart, Lisa, and Maggie, this means that we can make inferences about how healthy they are now and their opportunities to be healthy in the future, based on where they live.

Since the Simpson's Springfield does not exist, we can analyze county-level data for the forty-two US counties that have a town named Springfield. We standardized overall health rankings relative to state averages (it is methodologically hard to compare individual ranks across state lines) for health outcomes and health factors. Then we drilled down to consider risks of premature death by county.

| SPRINGFIELD, USA—COUNTIES WITH TOWNS NAMED SPRINGFIELD | | | |
|---|---|---|---|
| Conway, AR | Washington, KY | Union, NJ | Windsor, VT |
| Tuolumne, CA | Livingston, LA | Essex, NJ | Fairfax, VA |
| Baca, CO | Penobscot, ME | Ostego, NY | Albemarle, VA |
| Duval, FL | Hampden, MA | Clark, OH | Page, VA |
| Bay, FL | Calhoun, MI | Lane, OR | Westmoreland, VA |
| Effingham, GA | Brown, MN | Delaware, PA | Hampshire, WV |
| Bingham, ID | Greene, MO | Orangeburg, SC | Dane, WI |
| Sangamon, IL | Sarpy, NE | Bon Homme SD | Jackson, WI |
| LaPorte, IN | Sullivan, NH | Robertson, TN | St Croix, WI |
| Posey, IN | Burlington, NJ | Jim Wells, TX | Walworth, WI |

**TABLE 3.1. Springfield, USA—Counties with Towns and Cities Named Springfield**

*There are forty-two cities called "Springfield" in forty-two counties in thirty-seven states. Measuring health factors from Springfields across the US is neither a random sample nor a truly representative process. Some states, like Virginia and Wisconsin, are overrepresented. Other states, like Alaska, Hawaii, Nevada, and Washington, do not appear on the list. Even so, the populations of Springfield can illustrate the impact of social determinants of health on American families. Source: https://en.wikipedia.org/wiki/Springfield*

## HOMER IS FAT

Nicholas Christakis, a physician and social scientist, was a lecturer at my graduate school. He hypothesized that people are embedded in social networks and are influenced by the evident appearance and behaviors of those around them, suggesting that weight gain in one person might influence weight gain in others. Having obese social contacts might change a person's tolerance for being obese or might influence his or her adoption of specific behaviors (e.g., smoking, eating, and exercising). In addition to such strictly social mechanisms, it is plausible that physiological imitation might occur; areas of the brain that correspond to actions such as eating food may be stimulated if these actions are observed in others. In a landmark study, Christakis's group of researchers evaluated a network of 12,067 people living in small town in Massachusetts who underwent repeated measurements over a period of thirty-two years. They observed that people are embedded in social networks, suggesting that both bad and good behaviors might spread over a range of social ties. This highlights the necessity of approaching obesity not only as a clinical problem but also as a population health problem.[3]

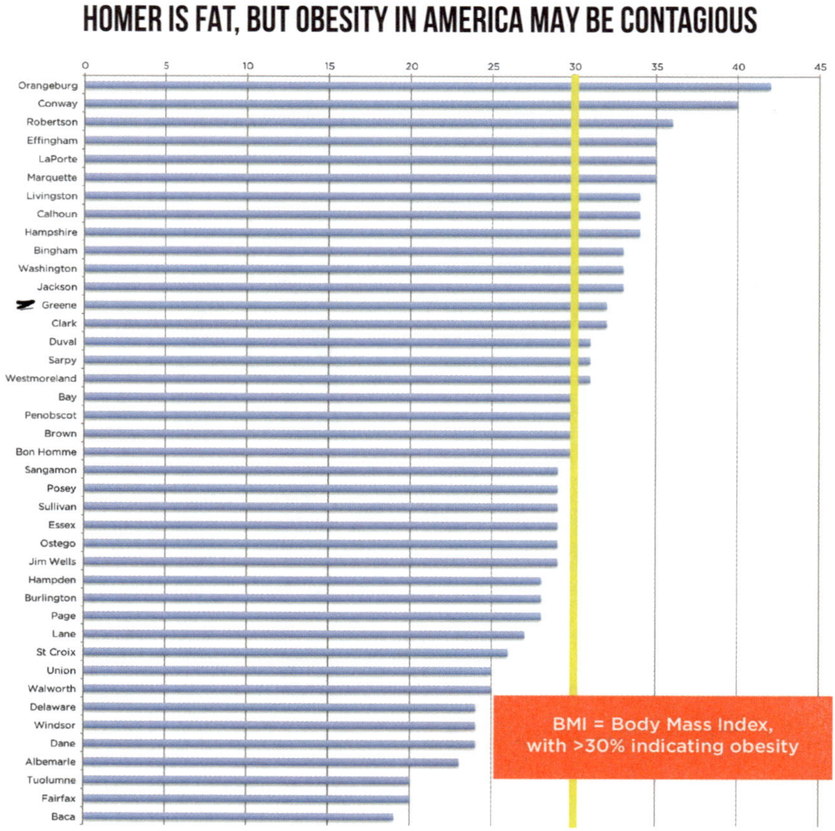

## HOMER IS FAT, BUT OBESITY IN AMERICA MAY BE CONTAGIOUS

**FIGURE 3.4. Obesity in America May Be Contagious**

*Adult obesity is defined as the percentage of the adult population that has a body mass index greater than or equal to thirty. More than two-thirds of all American adults are overweight or obese. Obesity is one of the biggest drivers of preventable chronic diseases in the US. However, our cities and our friends may be contributing to diet and exercise habits that make Americans fat. Some communities may tend to make Homer fatter, whereas some places are designed for exercise and are generally healthier. Source: www. countyhealthrankings.org*

In Homer's case, he is statistically more likely to be obese in some counties more than in others. It may be that his friends are helping to make him fatter! Christakis's research changed the way that physicians (and public health professionals) think about social networks, social support, and the connection between individual behaviors and population health outcomes. Since his article was published in 2007, other peer-reviewed articles have cited it more than 1,649 times.

The medical care costs of obesity in the United States are high. In 2008 dollars, these costs were estimated to be $147 billion. The annual nationwide productive costs of obesity-related absenteeism ranges between $3.38 billion ($79 per obese individual) and $6.38 billion ($132 per obese individual).

## MARGE IS WORRIED

Many people—mothers and fathers alike—worry about the safety of their neighborhood. Unsafe neighborhoods can cause anxiety, depression, and stress, and are linked to higher rates of pre-term births and low-birth-weight babies, even when income is accounted for. Fear of violence can keep people indoors, away from neighbors, exercise, and healthy foods. Companies may be less willing to invest in unsafe neighborhoods, making jobs harder to find. We can draw inferences about the safety of the Simpsons' neighborhood based on the incident of violence and injury deaths in their county.

# MARGE WORRIES ABOUT HER NEIGHBORHOOD: COMMUNITY SAFETY MATTERS

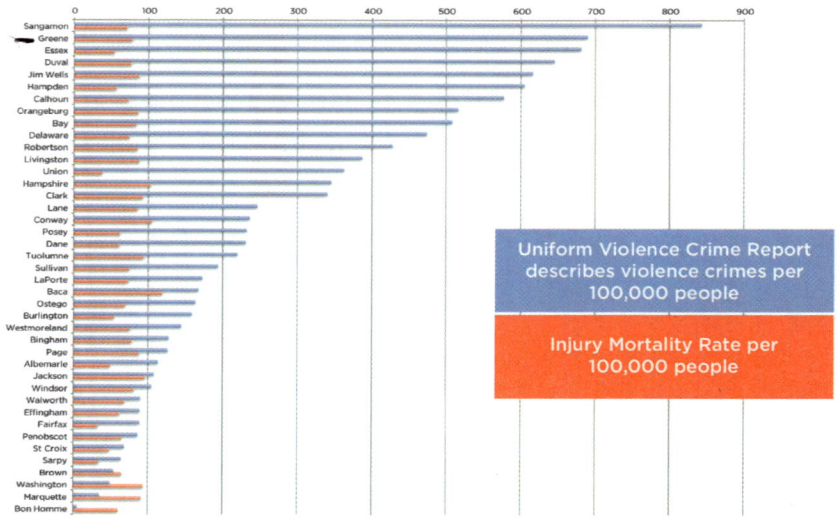

### FIGURE 3.5. Community Safety Matters for Families

*County Health Rankings associates unsafe communities with "anxiety, depression, and stress" as well as "higher rates of low birth weight babies, even when income is accounted for. Fear of violence can keep people indoors, away from neighbors, exercise, and healthy foods." Communities give mothers like Marge peace of mind by adopting policies to prevent accidents and violence. Source: www.countyhealthrankings.org*

Unsafe neighborhoods contribute to stress. Some states are more stressful to live in than others. But safe neighborhoods can reduce worry and anxiety. Protective neighborhoods offer social support, access to resources, and a sense of togetherness by encouraging community involvement and fostering healthy relationships across age and social groups. In recent years, a rapid rise in poor, densely populated urban neighborhoods that generally lack these protective features has put a great number of young people at risk for poor health. "The built environment might seem more public works than public health—but it's a factor that we should consider as a social determinant of health," says Dee Merriam, a community planner with the Healthy Community Design Initiative (HCDI). "The built environment is a term for the human-made landscape that we all live and work in," Merriam explains. "It includes parks, sidewalks, and a lot more—from buildings to boulevards, canopy trees to parking lots. A healthy community is one that enables people to make healthy choices as part of their day-to-day tasks."[4] We can design our communities to reduce stress and improve well-being.

## BART IS IN TROUBLE

The rise of disconnected youth, defined as those age sixteen to twenty-four who are not in school and not working, means that Bart has more opportunities to cause trouble. Youth disconnected from opportunity—meaning the chance to advance in school, gain work experience, form relationships, and build social supports in the community—represent untapped potential to strengthen the social and economic vibrancy of every Springfield. Bart is not the best student; truancy and a tendency to seek trouble are individual factors that may impact his ability to graduate high school. However, the opportunities in his community can be categorized by the prevalence of disconnected youth.

# BART MAY BE IN TROUBLE: OPPORTUNITIES FOR JOBS AND EDUCATION VARIES ACROSS SPRINGFIELDS

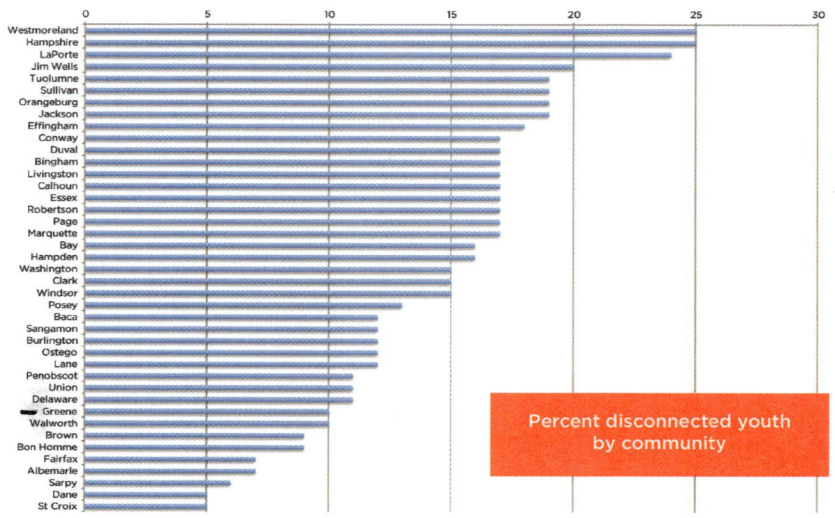

**FIGURE 3.6. Opportunity Varies with Local Circumstances**

*Youth disconnection illustrates the strength of connections between young adults and their community. County Health Ranks reports that disconnected youth "are at an increased risk of violent behavior, smoking, alcohol consumption, and marijuana use and may have emotional deficits and less cognitive and academic skill than their peers who are working and/or in school." In some US counties, Bart is five times more likely to be out of school and unemployed. It is a population health tragedy that rates of disconnected youth vary fivefold between healthy and unhealthy Springfields. Source: www.countyhealthrankings.org*

There are about 4.9 million young adults—one in eight—not working or in school. They are disconnected from opportunities to live long and healthy lives. Places with high levels of youth disconnection have higher rates of unemployment, child poverty, children in single-parent households, teen births, and lower educational attainment. Disconnected youth are very expensive in a community. The cost of each sixteen- to twenty-four-year-old disconnected youth is around $37,450 each year, when you include taxpayer burden and lost productivity.

## LISA LOVES SCHOOL

Good education predicts good health, and disparities in health and in educational achievement are closely linked. Why is it important to make sure as many students as possible end up with a high school diploma? Simply put: People who graduate from high school have better health than those who don't. In fact, research shows that education is one of the strongest predictors of long-term health.

An increase in formal education is consistently associated with lower death rates, whereas a decrease in education predicts earlier death. The less schooling people have, the higher their levels of risky health behaviors, such as smoking, being overweight, or having a low level of physical activity. High school completion is a useful measure of educational attainment because its influence on health is well studied, and it is widely recognized as the minimum entry requirement for higher education and well-paid employment.

And while the number of students dropping out of high school is decreasing, the problem is still dire. "Approximately 6,000 students daily are pushed out, pulled out or just give up on school," said Terri Wright, director of American Public Health Association's Center for School, Health, and Education.[5] In the US, about 1,000 high schools fail to graduate half their students, and in more than twenty cities at least three-quarters of high school students attend schools where fewer than 60 percent of students graduate.[6] There are major differences by county in the percentage of ninth graders who graduate high school in four years.

# LISA LOVES SCHOOL: HIGH SCHOOL GRADUATION RATES BY COUNTY

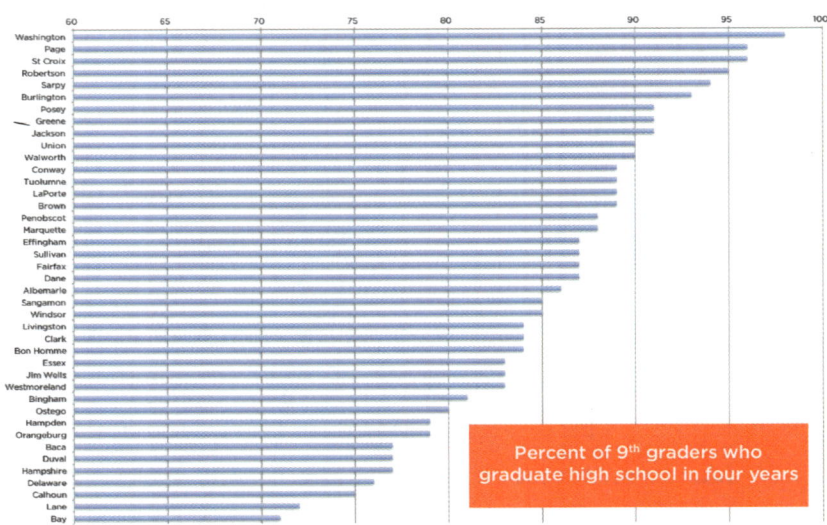

**FIGURE 3.7. High School Graduation Rates by County**

*There is a national push to prevent students from dropping out of high school. However, the local penetration of evidence-based programs to improve high school graduation varies county to county. Some areas have fully implemented effective transitions between middle school and high school, mentorship programs, career counseling, and technical education tracks. Source: www.countyhealthrankings.org*

One of the most common reasons for a high-achieving girl like Lisa to drop out is teen pregnancy. There are many evidence-based strategies that have been proven to reduce the number of young women, such as Lisa, who get pregnant before the age of nineteen. Compared with their peers who delay childbearing, teen girls who have babies are:

- less likely to finish high school

- more likely to rely on public assistance

- more likely to be poor as adults

- more likely to have children who have poorer educational, behavioral, and health outcomes over the course of their lives than do kids born to older parents

But different communities have very different rates of teen births.

## TEEN BIRTH RATES IMPACT INDIVIDUALS LIKE LISA AND COMMUNITIES LIKE SPRINGFIELD USA

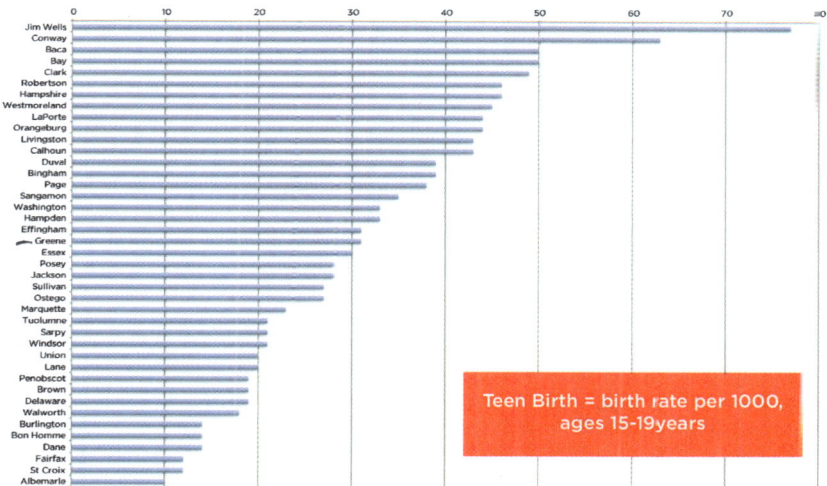

**FIGURE 3.8. Teen Birth Rates Impact Individuals and the Community**

*Depending on where the Simpsons live, Lisa may be eight times more like to have a child before she graduates high school than if she lived in a community with a comprehensive strategy to address reproductive health. Teen birth is defined as the birth rate per a thousand female population, ages fifteen to nineteen. Source: www.countyhealthrankings.org*

By ensuring teens graduate high school and delay pregnancy, we can help make our communities healthier.

## PROTECTING MAGGIE

One of the objectives of *Healthy People 2020*, the federal government's roadmap toward national health improvement, is to get the number of infant deaths in the United States down to sixty out of every ten thousand live births. Unfortunately, half of all Springfields in the United States have yet to reduce child mortality to an acceptable level.

## KEEPING MAGGIE SAFE — HOW CHILDHOOD MORTALITY VARIES ACROSS COUNTIES

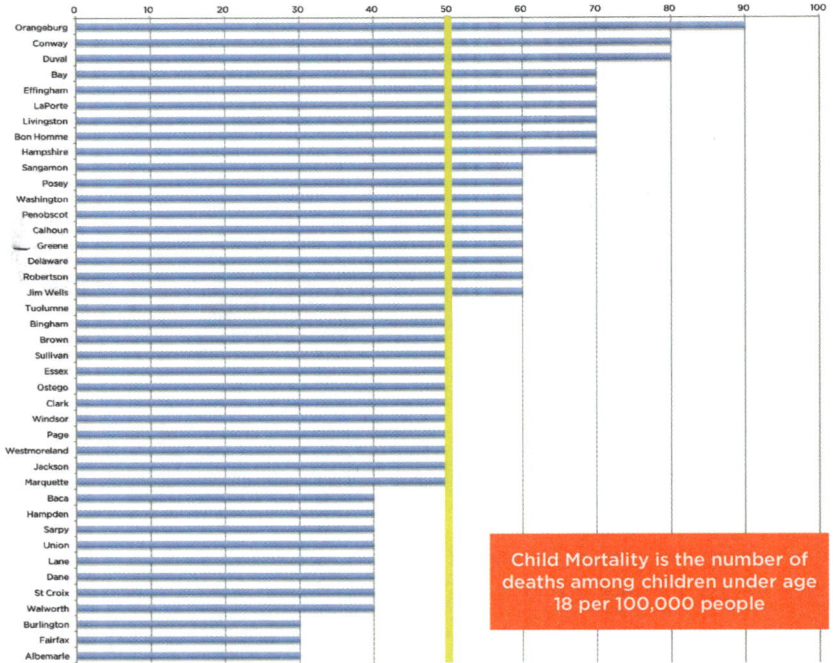

Child Mortality is the number of deaths among children under age 18 per 100,000 people

**FIGURE 3.9. Keeping Maggie Safe—How Childhood Mortality Varies across Counties**

*We all expect babies like Maggie to be born healthy, grow up in supportive homes, and survive their adolescence. However, the rates of childhood mortality vary widely by county. In some Springfields, Maggie is three times more likely to die before her*

*eighteenth birthday than in other similar cities. The community where Maggie lives, grows up, learns, and plays determines the differences in mortality. Source: www.coun-tyhealthrankings.org*

But keeping Maggie safe goes beyond just keeping her alive. Experiences in childhood are related to success, as well as struggle. Children from stable homes have better health outcomes than children from unstable homes, while difficult early life experiences are associated with criminality, illiteracy, poor economic participation, and poor relationships. Children from disadvantaged backgrounds are more likely to do poorly in school and, subsequently, as adults are more likely to have lower incomes and higher fertility rates, are less likely to be empowered or independent, and are more likely to struggle to provide good healthcare, nutrition, and stimulation for their own children, thus contributing to the intergenerational transmission of disadvantage.

Early life includes maternal health even before a child is born. Family planning, prenatal vitamins, and stable social situations prepare future mothers to have healthy children. Poor circumstances during pregnancy adversely affect a developing fetus. Poor nutrition, maternal stress, smoking, drug use, preventable infections, and alcohol use contribute to prematurity but also represent a risk to health later in life.

Adverse childhood experience can profoundly affect a child well into adulthood. Vincent Felitti taught a childhood development course at my medical school. At the time, I didn't recognize how lucky I was. In the mid-1980s, Felitti noted that the dropout rate for his obesity clinic was greater than 50 percent. He began to do structured interviews looking at 10 types of early childhood trauma: physical abuse, sexual abuse, emotional abuse, physical neglect, domestic violence in the home, parental substance abuse, parental divorce, incarceration of a family member, and family history of mental illness. Surprisingly, Felitti found that Adverse Childhood Experiences—he calls them ACEs—were common, often occurred together, and have dose-response relationships with many health problems. In a cohort of 13,934 adults recruited from Kaiser-Permanent HMO in Southern California (think employed, insured, high-functioning neighbors and friends you see at the supermarket), the presence of four or more ACEs in a child's life was strongly associated with adulthood high-risk health behaviors, including smoking, alcohol use, drug abuse, promiscuity, and severe obesity, as well as mental health issues, such as anxiety and depression. It might make sense that psychological trauma in a child would affect behavioral health later in life. However, Felitti also observed that ACEs were associated with increased risk of cancer, chronic lung disease, heart disease, stroke, liver disease, osteoporosis, diabetes, and premature death.[7] The results of the ACEs study have been replicated in more than fifty peer-reviewed papers. Felitti's questions—now called the ACE-IQ—has been incorporated into the Central for Disease Control Behavioral Risk Factor Surveillance System, an annual survey conducted by state departments across the US.

In recognition of the importance of early childhood experiences, there has been a surge of research and interest in early childhood interventions. It can be hard to find a program or intervention that is right for your community. However, there are many resources to help. For example, *Blueprints for Healthy Youth Development* provides a registry of evidence-based positive youth development programs designed to promote the health and well-being of children and teens. Blueprints programs are family, school, and community based and target all levels of need—from broad prevention programs that promote positive behaviors while decreasing negative behaviors, to highly-targeted programs for at-risk children and troubled teens that get them back on track. Hosted by the Center for the Study and Prevention of Violence at the University of Colorado Boulder, Blueprints has reviewed more than 1,400 programs, but fewer than 5 percent of them have been designated as model and promising programs.[8] These programs will help young people reach their full potential by promoting positive youth development, such as academic performance and success, emotional well-being, positive relationships, and physical health. Blueprints prevention and intervention programs also help young people overcome challenges associated with violence, delinquency, and substance abuse. More importantly, Blueprints publishes their findings publically. Blueprints help community leaders search and compare programs by problem behavior, education, emotional well-being, physical health, or positive relationships. The database provides an easy-to-use reference by program descriptions, target population, funding strategies, benefits, costs, and impact.

## SOCIAL DETERMINANTS HEALTH INFLUENCE IF A COMMUNITY IS HEALTHY OR SICK

The SDH are based on the social and environmental conditions where people live. Everyone lives somewhere along a social gradient: some families are more advantaged, with access to education, healthy food options, safe neighborhoods, nice houses, and rich social networks; some families are not. The poorest of the poor, around the world, have the worst health. Evidence shows that even within countries, the lower an individual's position is in society, the worse their health. There is a social gradient in health that runs from top to bottom of the socioeconomic spectrum. Michael Marmot led the decade long effort at the World Health Organization to build consensus toward action on the social determinants of health. In the landmark report *Closing the Gap in a Generation: Health Equity through Action on the Social Determinants of Health*, Marmot notes, "There are other factors that influence health, but these are outweighed by the overwhelming impact of social and economic factors—the material, social, political, and cultural conditions that shape our lives and our behaviors."[9]

## PARENTS WHO WANT TO LIVE IN A HEALTHY COMMUNITY HAVE TWO OPTIONS: MOVE OR GET ORGANIZED

Healthy communities lead to healthier families. Consider the *Move to Opportunity* study. In 1994, the US Department of Housing and Urban Development (HUD) randomized 4,600 low-income families to three groups: Group #1, move to a private-market house in a low-poverty neighborhood; Group #2, move to a traditional Section 8 apartment in a low-income area; or Control Group #3, stay in their current neighborhood. When researchers followed up ten years later, the outcomes were staggering.

When families from all three groups were surveyed, the researchers found major improvements in health and well-being for families who moved to low-poverty neighborhoods:

- Adults had improved physical health and lower rates of severe obesity and diabetes

- Adults had improved mental health, including lower rates of depression

- The differences in health and well-being were not explained by changes in income, child education, or other social factors (such as race and gender)

The families who used HUD vouchers to move to healthier neighborhoods became much healthier than families who stayed in rough neighborhoods.[10] Where you live affects your health, as demonstrated by the impact of different Springfield locations on the Simpson's family. Not every family has the opportunity to move to the healthier Springfield. But it is possible for families to advocate for healthy policies and programs in their hometown.

## REFLECTION QUESTIONS

1. Have you looked up the health outcomes of your county lately? Go to County Health Rankings (www. countyhealthrankings.org) and see how your community compares to other counties in your state.

2. Peer pressure can lead to good (or bad) health choices. Can you think of any cultural or social strength that you could harness to address the social determinants of health in your town?

3. Which Simpson's family members would struggle to be healthy in your community? Should you focus on helping Homer, Margie, Bart, Lisa, or Maggie first?

---

**PART 3 ENDNOTES**

1    Michael Blanding interviewing David Bloom. "Public Health and the US Economy." *Harvard TH Chan Magazine* (Fall 2012), www.hsph.harvard.edu/news/magazine/ public-health-economy-election/

2    Zachary Crockett, "What Homer Simpson's 100+ Jobs Tell Us about America's Middle Class," *Vox.com* (Sept 16, 2016), www.vox.com/2016/9/6/12752476/ the-simpsons-homer-middle-class

3    Nicholas A. Christakis and James H. Fowler, "The Spread of Obesity in a Large Social Network over 32 Years," *N Engl J Med* (2007): DOI: 10.1056/NEJMsa066082

4    Dee Merriam, "Designing, Planning and Building Healthy Communities." *CDC Blog* (Feb 2016), https://blogs.cdc.gov/yourhealthyourenvironment/2016/02/24/designing-planning-and-building-healthy-communities/

5    "High School Graduation," American Public Health Association, last modified 2017, https://www.apha.org/topics-and-issues/high-school-graduation

6    Christopher B. Swanson, "Who graduates? Who doesn't? A Statistical Portrait of Public High School Graduation, Class of 2001," The Urban Institute, last modified 2004, Washington, D.C., http://www.urban.org/UploadedPDF/410934_ Who-Graduates.pdf

7    Robert Anda, Valerie Edwards, Vincent Felitti, Mary Koss, James Marks, Dale Nordenberg, Alison Spitz, and David Williams, "Relationship of Childhood Abuse and Household Dysfunction to Many of the Leading Causes of Death in Adults: The Adverse Childhood Experiences (ACE) Study," *American Journal of Preventive Medicine* 14, no. 4 (May 1998): 245–258.

8    Blueprints Programs for Healthy Youth Development, http://www.blueprintsprograms.com

9    Michael Marmont et al., "Closing the Gap in a Generation: Health Equity through Action on the Social Detriments of Health," The Global Commission on Social Determinants of Health, WHO (2008). http://apps.who.int/iris/bitstream/10665/43943/1/9789241563703_eng.pdf

10   "Moving to Opportunity for Fair Housing," U.S. Department of Housing and Urban Development, 1996, https://portal.hud.gov/hudportal/HUD?src=/programdescription/mto

**PART 4**

# BUILDING HEALTHY COMMUNITIES

**CHALLENGE:** The design of our towns makes it hard for families to be healthy. Can we design our communities to make healthy choices easier for families?

It is hard for a family to be healthy in an average American city. There are a number of economic factors: wage stagnation, household debt, rising healthcare costs, tax burden, and weak public systems. When you ask parents what they want for themselves and their children, the answers are fairly consistent. Families want the opportunity to pursue the American Dream. Soon after President Barack Obama took office in 2009, he created a task force aimed at raising the living standards of the middle class. But first, the task force had to define middle class. The idea was to capture the multidimensional and individual notions of "being middle class" while emphasizing functional capabilities, social inclusion, relationships, the environment, and other components of well-being. How did Obama's focus group choose to define this group? Through their aspirations, which was fitting for the "Yes We Can" president. For Aspirational Middle Class, the most important characteristics were the basic priorities for living the American Dream: own a home, take yearly vacations, own a car, afford financial and retirement security, and to send the kids to college.[1]

Health inequality refers to the difference in health between families who achieve the American Dream and families who don't. People have poorer health and die younger based on the circumstances they are in, communities where they live, and what they do as part of their day-in-day-out routine. This social gradient is not rooted in some absolute, yes/no types of differences, like lack of school or available jobs in their community. The gaps tend to emerge based on relative factors: such as poor education at an underfunded school or unstable employment in a hazardous workplace. People from lower-socioeconomic-level communities have shorter life expectancies and higher risk of life-threatening illnesses. It turns out, the opportunity to achieve the American Dream depends as much as the neighborhood and the community where a family lives as any other factor.

## WHAT IF MOTHER WERE MAYOR?

If it takes a healthy town for a family to thrive, then I believe mother should be mayor. My grandmother, Barbara Fleming, was an amazing woman. She taught English-as-a-Second-Language, coached the city championship baseball team, served on the city counsel, and was elected mayor of Willows, CA, in the 1960s. She also managed to raise five high-energy children. But Gram—I called her Gram and my grandfather was "Pa," like Gram-Pa—was a polio survivor who spent her adult life in a wheelchair. Female, disabled, and empowered. As mayor, she defended free speech and advocated for green spaces. At the time, there was a debate about what to do with multiple acres of undeveloped city land: sell it to real estate developers, build more administrations buildings, or maybe lease it to local businesses. My grandmother, the mayor, championed an effort to convert the land into Sycamore Park. The public-access recreational area now has a playground, exercise track, giant trees, community center, horseshoe pits, and even a skateboard park. The green space connects the downtown, elementary school, junior high, and multiple neighborhoods. Barbara Fleming—my Gram—lived in Willows for fifty-six years. She did not have the option to move, so she made sure the town was built for healthy living: not just for her family, but for everyone. When mothers are mayors, towns make better decisions about health.

The *California Health In All Policies* taskforce pulled together leaders from government agencies and local communities to ask the key question: what do you want your community to look like? The goal was to get input from community members and eighteen different state agencies on how programs, policies, and strategies could strengthen communities. They produced a list of core domains for a healthy community, and descriptions of what the community would look like. I adapted it to include examples of policies that have evidence to support the goals, and resources to look up additional evidence-based strategies to make communities healthy. This is the type of town, county, or state where parents want to raise children.

# FAMILIES ENVISION HEALTHY COMMUNITIES

When we build healthy communities, we need to remember that the community must:

- #1: Meet the basic needs of all.

- #2: Embrace sustainable environmental policy.

- #3: Promote economic and social development.

- #4: Foster social relationships that are supportive and respectful.

Healthy communities that put the needs and priorities of families first will benefit from examples of health in all policies, metrics to track progress, and best-practice registries to gain inspiration.

## #1—MEET THE BASIC NEEDS OF ALL

| HEALTHY COMMUNITIES MEET THE BASIC NEEDS OF ALL | | | | |
|---|---|---|---|---|
| **CORE DOMAIN** | **DESCRIPTION** | **EXAMPLES** | **METRICS** | **BEST PRACTICE REGISTRIES** |
| **MEET THE BASIC NEEDS OF ALL** | Transportation | Traffic Calming; Universal Helmet Laws; Complete Streets Policy | The percentage of the work force driving alone who spend more than 30 minutes commuting to work is measured in long commute–driving alone. | Community Transportation Association of America: http://communitytrans-portationmarket-place.com |
| | Food | Coordinated Approach to Child Health (CATCH); 500 Club; WIC | Food environment index, an index of equally weighted factors that contribute to a healthy food environment, including limited access to healthy foods and food insecurity. | TheCommuni-tyGuide.org |
| | Clean Water | CDC Safe Water Program; Fluoridation | Drinking water violations is an indicator of the presence of health-related drinking water violations in a county. | EPA Drinking Water Systems: https://www.epa.gov/dwreginfo/information-about-public-water-systems |

**TABLE 4.1. Healthy Communities Meet the Basic Needs of All**

The stress of unmet basic needs leads many families to struggle with adverse health outcomes, both physical and mental. Basic needs are: food, water, housing, healthcare, and exercise. Chronic illness is more likely to affect those who live in resource-deprived neighborhoods, places where meeting basic needs is a day-to-day struggle. Children born to mothers who lack basic needs start out disadvantaged in life: they tend to be born earlier, be smaller, and are sicker than their matched counterparts from neighborhoods where basic needs are addressed.

Through a deep dive into social data, researchers show life expectancy for males at birth in different neighborhoods.[2] On the X-axis, there is a measure of relative neighborhood deprivation, which is associated with a lack of basic necessities (food, water, housing healthcare, or exercise). The most-deprived babies are shown on the left, and the least-deprived babies on the right. However, when you separate life expectancy by relative income, a starling trend emerges. Black dots represent children born to upper-income homes. Green dots are children born into impoverished families. It is well established that rich people are healthier and live longer than poor people. But there are two subtle but important messages hidden in this graph.

# HEALTHY NEIGHBORHOODS IMPROVE LIFE EXPECTANCY FOR EVERYONE—RICH & POOR

Life expectancy by US county, 2014

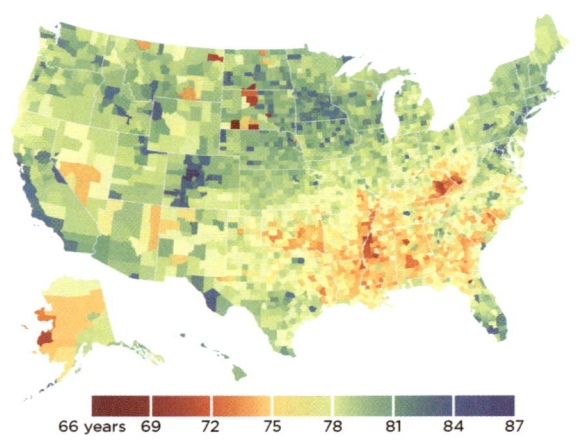

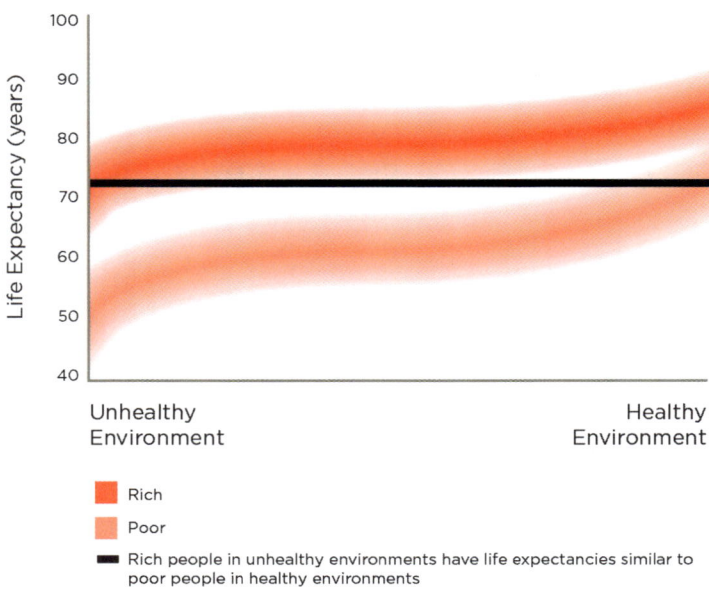

Rich people in unhealthy environments have life expectancies similar to poor people in healthy environments

**FIGURE 4.1. Life Expectancy Is Strongly Influenced by Relative Neighborhood Deprivation, Whether You Are Rich or Poor**

*Everyone tends to live longer in a healthy environment. However, longitudinal studies*

*in the UK and Canada have shown that poor families benefit more when they live with resource-rich neighborhoods. In fact, many poor families in resource-rich neighborhoods live longer than rich families in bad neighborhoods. Rich or poor, everyone fares better in a good neighborhood.*

## Reductions in Inequality Help Everyone, Even the Rich

Take home #1: Rich or poor, health is better and children live longer in the communities with even distributions of basic needs—on the right of the graph. As we can see, Health for All is not zero-sum nor is it transactional. When equity improves, health improves for everyone. The life expectancy of wealthy families is better when basic needs for all are routinely addressed.

## Increase in Inequality Hurts the Rich, But It Hits Working Families Harder

Take home #2: the health outcomes and life expectancy of rich people in the most deprived neighborhoods (on the left) were worse than poor children in equitable neighborhoods (on the right). So, even if you are wealthy, your money does not protect you from the negative health impacts of your neighbors lacking basic needs. However, a lack of wealth can be devastating where neighborhoods are deprived. If we want to address the basic needs of all, then we must have a Health in All policies approach to housing, employment, transportation, food, water, and exercise.

## Housing—Even a Little Housing Goes a Long Way

Massachusetts's Home and Healthy for Good Program, which housed 981 chronically homeless individuals in supportive housing, showed that in the six months prior to receiving housing, participants accumulated 1,812 emergency department visits, 3,163 overnight hospital stays, 847 ambulance rides, and 2,494 detox stays. The estimated total cost-per-person for measured services—including Medicaid ($26,124), shelter ($5,723), and incarceration ($1,343)—amounted to $33,190 per year. With the cost of housing and services through the HHG program amounting to $15,468 per tenant, the total estimated return on investment to the state was $9,118 per person.[3] For housing advocates, it makes no sense to accept the absurd cost to communities for failing to pay for adequate shelter for its most vulnerable families.

Community Solutions, a creative, mission-driven nonprofit that seeks to end homelessness and the conditions that create it, has shown that communities can bring the chronic homeless rate to zero. Zero; nada; no one stays homeless for more than thirty days, ever. Their *100K Homes* campaign has measured the cost to communities and concluded that US cities can no longer afford homelessness. Their website boasts, "Homelessness is a solvable problem that has lost its sense of urgency. Built for Zero is a rigorous national change effort designed to help a core group of committed US communities end chronic and veteran homelessness." However, this is not an empty claim. 100K Homes has worked with community leaders to adopt proven practices, deploy existing resources more efficiently, and utilize real-time IT solutions to measurably and sustainably end veteran homelessness in five major cities. In the last four years, the 100K Homes campaign has provided safe housing options for 105,580 families. The keys to their success include no-wrong-door services, housing-first policies, and coordinating housing services across community agencies so that staff of community organizations are able to connect families with the appropriate services in a manner that is streamlined, effective, and seamless from the family's perspective, even if the needed service is not offered by their organization or within their sector.[4, 5]

## Transportation—Designing Communities for Safe, Active Travel

The Robert Wood Johnson Foundation highlights the importance of transportation as a social determinant of health. Our current transportation system is a web of highways, bridges, roads, streets, and parking lots that are optimized for cars, trucks, vans, and SUVs, prioritizing individual freedom and personal vehicles. However, our culture of driving leads to some staggering health consequences: There were more than 32,000 crash deaths in the US each year. These deaths cost more than $380 million in direct medical costs. Air pollution (smog) leads to asthma exacerbations, cardiovascular disease, pre-term births, and premature death. Long-term, each additional hour spent in a car per day is associated with a 6 percent increase in likelihood of obesity.

As our communities sprawl, it becomes more difficult to access basic services without a personal automobile. Elderly, disabled, poor, and socially isolated individuals may not be able to pick up groceries, drive to a doctors appointment, vote, or have access to public parks without help. In many areas, public transportation is inadequate to meet to basic needs of vulnerable populations. From a purely medical perspective, transportation becomes a barrier to good healthcare. Transportation barriers lead to rescheduled or missed appointments, delayed care, and missed or delayed medication use. These consequences may lead to poorer management of chronic illness and, thus, poorer health outcomes. Cars can make us sick, yet in our car-optimized society, lack of a car can keep us from getting well.

## Safe Water—Learn from Flint

We tend to think of safe water as a problem for villages in Africa or South America. Safe water is relegated to a "poverty problem" or "third world issues." However, safe water from the tap is real problem relevant to US communities. A recent study estimates that contaminants in drinking water sicken up to 1.1 million people per year. Improper medicine disposal, chemical, pesticide, and microbiological contaminants in water can lead to poisoning, gastro-intestinal illnesses, eye infections, increased cancer risk, and many other health problems. The Flint water crisis is a reminder to all of us that supplying water is all about public health, and that the most vulnerable in our communities are the ones at greatest risk.

It was a pediatrician who initially identified the problem with Flint's water supply. Mona Hanna-Attisha connected problems in her young patients with the systemic water problem. She says, "Lead is a potent known neurotoxin. The CDC, the AAP, everybody tells us that there is no safe level of lead. Lead poisoning affects your cognition and your behavior."[6] Economist Peter Muennig with Columbia School of Public Health notes: "Each year in America there are roughly 90,000 low-level [lead] exposures, which commonly result from sources such as drinking water. These exposures rob children of IQ points, leading to lower economic productivity, higher welfare use, and additional criminal justice system costs." But the crisis in Flint was different. Muennig calculated that "there were more than 8,000 documented exposures, with the costs amounting to about $400 million and 1,760 quality-adjusted life-years lost."[7] The use of public water exposed the residents to excess amounts of lead after city planners changed the water source without input from the community.

# #2—EMBRACE SUSTAINABLE ENVIRONMENTAL POLICY

| CORE DOMAIN | DESCRIPTION | EXAMPLES | METRICS | BEST PRACTICE REGISTRIES |
|---|---|---|---|---|
| | | HEALTHY COMMUNITIES EMBRACE SUSTAINABLE ENVIRONMENTAL POLICY | | |
| EMBRACE SUSTAINABLE ENVIRONMENTAL POLICY | Healthcare | CHIP, Medicaid, and Medicare | Uninsured is defined as the percentage of the population younger than age 65 without health insurance. The data for this measure come from the Census Bureau's Small Area Health Insurance Estimates (SAHIE). The ratio of population to primary care physicians in a county (i.e., the number of people per primary care physician), the ratio of population to dentists in a county. Preventable hospital stays is the hospital discharge rate for ambulatory care-sensitive conditions per 1,000 fee-for-service Medicare enrollees. | Cochrane Collaboration |
| | Reproductive Health | RECAP, School-based Programs | Teen births, defined as the birth rate per 1,000 female population ages 15-19, as measured and provided by the National Center for Health Statistics (NCHS). Sexually transmitted infections, defined as the chlamydia rate per 100,000 population, as provided by the Centers for Disease Control and Prevention (CDC). | http://nahic.ucsf edu/wp-content/ uploads/2014/08/ Evidence-Based-Guide.pdf  http://www.etr. org/recapp/ |
| | Behavioral Health | Menta Health First Aid, Methadone Clinics, CBT, Suicide Prevention Resource Center | The ratio of population to mental health providers in a county. Suicides and drug overdoses per 100,000. Excessive drinking from the Behavioral Risk Factor Surveillance System (BRFSS). Alcohol-impaired driving deaths, defined as the percentage of driving deaths with alcohol involvement, as provided by the Fatality Analysis Reporting System. | https://www. samhsa.gov/ebp-web-guide  https://www. campbellcollaboration.org |

| | Exercise | Safe Routes to School; Rails-to-Trails Bicycle Paths; Walkability Index | Access to exercise opportunities, defined as the percentage of the population who live reasonably close to locations for physical activity, including parks or recreational facilities. | TheCommunityGuide.org |
|---|---|---|---|---|
| EMBRACE SUSTAINABLE ENVIRONMENTAL POLICY | Tobacco | Community Air Risk Evaluation (CARE) Program; Smoke-Free Zones | Behavioral Risk Factor Surveillance System (BRFSS) provided by the CDC reports the number of current adult smokers who have smoked at least 100 cigarettes in their lifetime. | TheCommunityGuide.org |
| | Sustainable Energy | Integrated Pest Management; Renewal Utilities; Pharmaceutical Diversion Programs; Life Cycle Design | Air pollution-particulate matter is defined as the average daily measure of fine particulate matter in micrograms per cubic meter (PM2.5) in a county. | PracticeGreenhealth.org |

**TABLE 4.2. Healthy Communities Embrace Sustainable Environmental Policy**

There are hundreds of examples of sustainable community projects across the United States. Such projects occur in all types of communities—in large, medium, and small cities; in towns; in counties; and in rural communities. Protective neighborhoods offer social support, access to resources, and a sense of togetherness by encouraging community involvement and fostering healthy relationships across age and social groups. In recent years, a rapid rise in poor, densely populated urban neighborhoods that generally lack these protective features puts a great number of young people at risk for poor health. Seattle has defined "sustainability" as "the long-term social, economic, and environmental health of our community . . . a sustainable city thrives without compromising the ability of future generations to meet their needs."[8] Neighborhoods must prosper within the web of the city. From public policy to individual lifestyles, leaders in sustainable communities must consider the effects that decisions are likely to have on the entire system—economic, social, and environmental—and on future generations.

As of 2014, some 40 million people—one in eight Americans—had been diagnosed with asthma.[9] Air pollution is associated with increased asthma rates and can aggravate asthma, emphysema, chronic bronchitis, and other lung diseases; damage airways and lungs; and increase the risk of premature death from heart or lung disease. Using 2009 data, the CDC's Tracking Network calculates that a 10 percent reduction in fine particulate matter could prevent more than 13,000 deaths per year in the US.[10]

Poor surface-water quality can also make lakes unsafe for swimming and wild fish unsafe for consumption. Nitrogen pollution and harmful algae blooms create toxins in water, which can lead to rashes, stomach or liver illness, respiratory problems, and neurological effects when people ingest or come into contact with polluted water. Water pollution also threatens wildlife habitats.

Many communities are choosing to pursue healthy energy policies to improve water and air quality. There are significant health tradeoffs involved in energy production. Cities and counties have options: fossil fuels, nuclear power, and renewable energy. Fossil fuels have serious implications for human health and healthy communities.[11] Fossil fuel extraction and consumption contribute to both local and global pollution. These health impacts accrue into a heavy and largely unaccounted-for economic burden born by communities, governments, and health systems. Six decades of nuclear power production has resulted in adverse health effects in workers in the nuclear fuel cycle, disastrous accidents that lead to widespread environmental contamination, and the unresolved problems of permanent and secure storage of high-level radioactive wastes.[12] Communities should carefully consider the tradeoffs of nuclear power, fossil fuels, and renewable energy when choosing a sustainable energy policy. Renewable energy sources, such as wind and solar, still require public health considerations. They have been associated with noise pollution and waste disposal. Hydroelectric power can have significant negative impacts on vulnerable communities. However, their overall population health burdens are much lower than for fossil fuels. Substantial public health benefits can be realized with a shift toward clean, renewable energy options.[13] Cities and counties will be healthier if they choose sustainable energy policies.[14] A transition to clean renewable energy will reduce the burden of disease from local pollution, minimize occupational hazards, and promote population health.

Many US cities have decided that choosing sustainable energy policies is the smart choice. The list is long. In summer 2017, more than a hundred cities committed to be powered by 100 percent renewable fuels. Examples of communities that have led the push towards sustainable energy include: Arlington, VA; Atlanta, GA; Baltimore, MD; Boulder, CO; Brownville, TX; Charlottesville, VA; Chattanooga, TN; Chicago, IL; Cleveland, OH; Curry County, OR; Ithaca, NY; Pico Union, CA; Minneapolis, MN; New Bedford, MA; New Haven, CT; New York, NY; Olympia, WA; Portland, OR; San Francisco, CA; San Jose, CA; Sarasota, FL; Seattle, WA; Waterloo, IA; and Zuni, NM.[15] I love this list because it highlights cities big and small, north and south, east and west, Republican and Democrat, red state and blue state, conservative and progressive.

# #3—PROMOTE ECONOMIC AND SOCIAL DEVELOPMENT

| | HEALTHY COMMUNITIES PROMOTE ECONOMIC AND SOCIAL DEVELOPMENT | | | |
| CORE DOMAIN | DESCRIPTION | EXAMPLES | METRICS | BEST PRACTICE REGISTRIES |
| --- | --- | --- | --- | --- |
| PROMOTE ECONOMIC AND SOCIAL DEVELOPMENT | Jobs | Living Wage Laws, Paid Family Leave, Transitional Jobs, Vocation Training for Young Adults | The annual average unemployment rate: the total unemployed persons, as a percentage of the civilian labor force ages 16 and older. Income inequality—the ratio of household income at the 80th percentile level with that at the 20th percentile from the American Community Survey. | What Works Wisconsin: http:/fyi.uwex.edu/whatworkswisconsin/ |

**TABLE 4.3. Healthy Communities Promote Economic and Social Development**

It is true: having a job is better than having no job. Work means income. Fulfilling work translates work into a sense of identity, self-worth, and sense of accomplishment. Income allows people to obtain basic life necessities as well as productively contribute to their community. For work to be fulfilling, there are three major requirements. Workers need a degree of autonomy appropriate to their skill level and talents. Workers need clear connections between daily tasks and meaningful outcomes to be happy at work. Finally, fulfilling work places an individual's effort within a community context, so that a job well done rewards the individual and enriches the society. People who work have better health; people who report feeling fulfilled at work are happy and healthy.

## Income: It Is More than Just Money

Income is closely linked to social status and health outcomes. Social status refers to the pecking order in a society. It is often assumed and not polite to talk about money at the dinner table. If you are wondering about someone's income, then you may ask about their profession. We use professions as a proxy for income and social class in the America. As an example, how would your favorite aunt answer this question: "Would you be more likely to brag to your hairdresser that her nephew is a: 1) doctor, 2) social worker, 3) CEO, 4) receptionist,  5) construction worker, 6) soldier, 7) yoga instructor, 8) DMV clerk, or 9) street performer?" There is an implicit rank involved in different professions. At the heart of our concern for social status (and also social mobility) is a desire to create conditions where people can lead flourishing lives. People need to have control over their lives, and communities need to know that children, parents, and grandparents will thrive.

In a landmark study, the previously mentioned Michael Marmot enrolled eighteen thousand male civil servants in the UK, ages twenty to sixty-four, then followed up their health outcomes over the next ten years.[16] The name of the study—Whitehall—refers to the nickname for British Civil Corps taken from a set of Tudor buildings on Whitehall Street in London. On paper, in the UK it is possible to stratify, from low to high, every civil servant based on a pay scale that correlates with responsibility, function, and influence. From the beginning, it was clear where each of the ten thousand participants were in the pecking order. Participants were asked questions about risk factors for developing disease (such as obesity and smoking), leisure time, physical activity, underlying illness, blood pressure, and even height. The investigators controlled for these behavioral and genetic factors in their analysis. In addition, all civil servants had access to free healthcare, thus minimizing the role of access to healthcare as an explanation for difference. The result? A steep inverse association between income and health and mortality from a wide range of diseases, including heart disease, some cancers, chronic lung disease, depression, suicide, back pain, and even sick days. After controlling for all the factors, low-level employees were twice as likely to die of cardiovascular disease as were high-level leaders. Following up on Marmot's work in England, researchers in Canada estimated the economic impact if the health status and healthcare utilization patterns of lower-class groups equaled those of middle-class families. If lower-class groups had the same health status as middle-class families, then the healthcare gains would enable greater participation in the economy. Reducing the cost of lost productivity by only 10 percent could add billions of dollars to the Canadian economy![17]

## Inequality Makes You Sick! The Gini Index and Health

The Gini index is a measure of the distribution of a region's residents, and is the most commonly used measure of inequality. The Gini index varies between zero and one. A value of one indicates perfect inequality, where only one household has any income. A value of zero indicates perfect equality, where all households have equal income. Income inequality affects how long and how well we live and is particularly harmful to the health of poorer individuals.

Income inequality within US communities can have broad health impacts, including increased risk of mortality, poor health, and increased cardiovascular disease risks. Inequalities in a community can accentuate differences in social class and status and serve as a social stressor. Communities with greater income inequality can experience a loss of social connectedness, as well as decreases in trust, social support, and a sense of community for all residents. When we compare life expectancy in other countries, we see a strong correlation between income inequality and health.

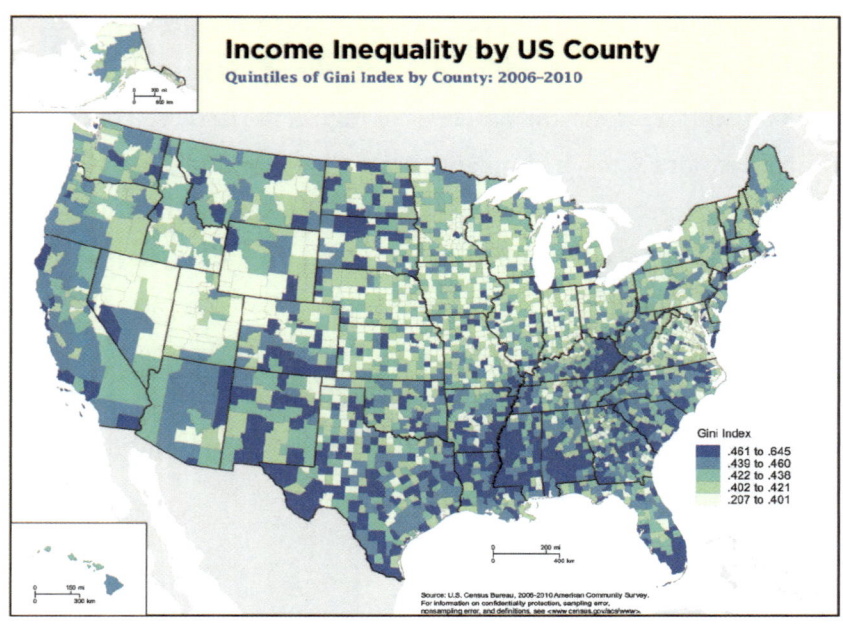

Income Inequality by US County

Quintiles of Gini Index by County: 2006–2010

Gini Index
.461 to .645
.439 to .460
.422 to .438
.402 to .421
.207 to .401

Source: U.S. Census Bureau, 2006–2010 American Community Survey.
For information on confidentiality protection, sampling error,
nonsampling error, and definitions, see <www.census.gov/acs/www>.

**FIGURE 4.2. Income Inequality by US County: Quintiles of Gini Index by County 2006–2010**

*Researchers have noted, "Adults in the highest income brackets are healthier than those in the middle class and will live, on average, more than six years longer than those with the lowest incomes."[18] Gini index is a measure of income inequality. The Gini index varies between zero and one. A value of one indicates perfect inequality where only one household has any income. A value of zero indicates perfect equality, where all households have equal income. The American Community Survey demonstrates that county-level Gini indexes ranged from 0.645 (high inequality) to 0.207 (low inequality). Source: American Community Survey Briefs 2012*

There is a statistically significant correlation between income inequality and life expectancy in the US. Even more surprising is that the difference in life expectancy is not due to being poor. Wealthy people in communities with high inequality do not live as long as wealthy people with high equality! When University of Wisconsin researchers at the Population Health Institute looked at county health rankings data to evaluate the impact of income inequity on life expectancy, they were shocked.

## U.S. LIFE EXPECTANCY VS. INEQUALITY, 2010

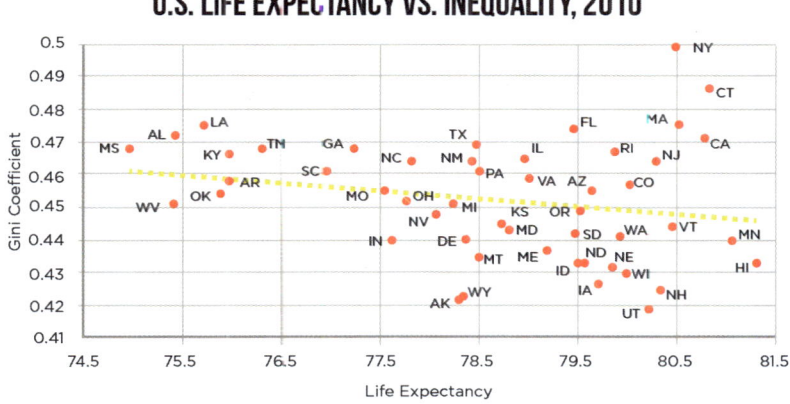

**FIGURE 4.3. What Is the Relationship between Income Inequality and Health in the United States?**

*High levels of income inequality are associated with lower life expectancy. Poor health and poverty do go hand in hand. But high levels of inequality negatively affect the health of even the affluent, because inequality fractures community cohesion and leads to stress, fear, and insecurity for everyone. Source: www.inequality.org*

For every one-point increase in the ratio between high and low earners in a county, there were about five years lost for every one thousand people. As one health commentator put it, "That's about the same difference they observed when a community's smoking rate increased by 4 percent or its obesity rate rose by 3 percent."[19] Adequate social and economic support increases life expectancy. The truth is that good friends and a stable job are equally important to health as avoiding bad habits like overeating, sedentary lifestyle, or smoking.

# #4 - FOSTER SOCIAL RELATIONSHIPS THAT ARE SUPPORTIVE AND RESPECTFUL

| HEALTHY COMMUNITIES FOSTER SOCIAL RELATIONSHIPS THAT ARE SUPPORTIVE AND RESPECTFUL | | | | |
|---|---|---|---|---|
| **CORE DOMAIN** | **DESCRIPTION** | **EXAMPLES** | **METRICS** | **BEST PRACTICE REGISTRIES** |
| **FOSTER SOCIAL RELATIONSHIPS THAT ARE SUPPORTIVE AND RESPECTFUL** | Childcare | Early Head Start, Child Care Subsidies, Advocates for Youth | Children in poverty--the percentage of children living in poverty, as defined by the federal poverty threshold--based on data from the Census' Small Area Income and Poverty Estimates (SAIPE) as well as Children in single-parent households is defined as the percentage of children living in family households who are raised by a single parent. These data come from the American Community Survey. | Blueprints for Health Youth Development: http://www.blueprintsprograms.com |
| | Education | Knowledge is Power Program (KIPP) | High school graduation is the percentage of the ninth grade cohort that graduates high school in four years. Disconnected youth from Measure of America and the American Community Survey. | What Works Clearinghouse |
| | Elder Care | Aging and Disability Resource Center (ADRC); Elder Justice Coalition | Social associations is defined as the number of membership associations per 10,000 population. This county-level measure is calculated from the County Business Patterns. | www.eldercare.gov |
| | Civic Engagement | Getting Equity Advocacy Results (GEAR) | Social associations is defined as the number of membership associations per 10,000 population. This county-level measure is calculated from the County Business Patterns. | policylink.org |
| | Safety | Restorative Justice, Community-Centered Policing Tools | The rate of violent crime per 100,000 population as reported to FBI's Uniform Crime Database. Injury deaths, defined as the injury mortality rate per 100,000 population using mortality data from CDC WONDER. | TheCommunityGuide.org; National Crime Prevention Council; https://www.crimesolutions.gov |

**TABLE 4.4. Healthy Communities Foster Social Relationships that are Supportive and Respectful**

Healthy and supportive relationships start at home, and extend into the community. Our first relationships with our parents have lasting health implications. When researchers randomized toddlers to receive weekly supervised play sessions with mothers, and then followed up the children as adolescents, the results were striking. Participants who played with their mom had lower rates of anxiety, depression, poor self-esteem, and anti-social behavior than children who did not participate in play session.[20] A massive amount of research has gone on to demonstrate that social exclusion later in life, including poverty, relative deprivation, and stigma, has major impacts on health. Mother Teresa famously said:

> We think sometimes that poverty is only being hungry, naked, and homeless. The poverty of being unwanted, unloved, and uncared for is the greatest poverty. We must start in our own homes to remedy this kind of poverty.[21]

Poverty also denies people access to house, education, and basic necessities for life. The inequality leads to worse health outcomes for vulnerable families, minorities, and stigmatized populations. Socially isolated individuals have an increased risk for poor health outcomes. Individuals who lack adequate social support are particularly vulnerable to the effects of stress, which has been linked to cardiovascular disease and unhealthy behaviors, such as overeating and smoking in adults, and obesity in children and adolescents. Adolescents are more protected from risk behaviors when they have friends who have strong social relationships and who model good health and health behaviors. The extent of peer influence, both positive and negative, has greatly expanded in recent years because of communication and interaction provided through social networking and media.

Social exclusion as a result of racism, discrimination, and stigmatization prevents people from accessing key services, including public health programs and healthcare, as well as participating in politics and community organizations. Disenfranchised, disempowered, and defenseless, socially excluded groups suffer from toxic stress and chronic insecurity, leading to worse health outcomes.[22]

Adopting and implementing policies and programs that support relationships between individuals and across entire communities can benefit health. Emphasizing efforts to support disadvantaged families and neighborhoods, where small improvements can have the greatest impacts, may make the greatest health improvements. In his Pulitzer prize-winning book, *Bowling Alone*, author and social scientist Robert Putnam draws on evidence including nearly five hundred thousand interviews over the last quarter-century to show that we sign fewer petitions, belong to fewer organizations that meet, know our neighbors less, meet with friends less frequently, and even socialize with our families less often.[23] In the late 1990s, Putnam wryly observed, "People watch *Friends* on TV—they don't have them in person."[24] Putnam shows how changes in work, family structure, age, suburban life, television, computers, women's roles, and other factors have contributed to this decline. His next book, *Better Together,* highlights a dozen case studies of successful community-building efforts in the United States. It is a collection of "exceptional cases in which creative social entrepreneurs move against the nationwide tide and create vibrant new forms of social connectedness." Putnam says, "We focus on these social-capital success stories hoping and believing that they may in fact be harbingers of a broader revival of social capital in this country."[25] The point is that even though social support in American may be declining, there are concrete steps communities can take and are taking to prevent social exclusion and to promote strong social supports.

## WHO BENEFITS FROM A HEALTHIER COMMUNITY?

So far, we have emphasized the benefits to families from a healthier community. However, the biggest impact of an integrated population health strategy coordinated across sectors will be shared between community organizations (save money) and families (live healthier).

For population health to matter, it must be meaningful to the families living in your community. A strong collaboration between community partners is not enough; the collaboration should and must translate into a better experience, better services, and better health: a Healthy Community. We can use the economic, political, technological, and scientific levers to advance health where people live, work, learn, and play.

## REFLECTION QUESTIONS

1.  How are healthy community initiatives held together?

2.  What is your Healthy Community elevator speech? Can you explain the benefits in thirty seconds to complete stranger? How else might you build shared value?

3.  Reflect on Warren Buffett's challenge to manage today like you have to live with your decisions for the next fifty years. What demographic factors will drive change in your community? Project these factors five to ten years into the future. What opportunities for your health will these demographic shifts create?

---

**PART 4 ENDNOTES**

1   "Annual Report of the White House Task Force on the Middle Class," Middle Class Task Force, February 2010.

2    Olugbenga Olatunde, Michael Smith, and Chris White, "Inequalities in Disability-Free Life Expectancy by Area Deprivation: England, 2001-04 and 2005-08," *Health Stat Q* 48, 36-57, Winter 2010.

3    Massachusetts Housing and Shelter Alliance, "Permanent Supportive Housing: A Solution-Driven Model," *Home & Healthy for Good Progress*, January 2015. http://www.mhsa.net/sites/default/files/January%202015%20HHG%20Report.pdf

4    Wendy Anderson, "What do 'No Wrong Door' and 'Warm Hand Off' Really Mean?" Children and Youth Services Network, Aug 19, 2013, accessed Sept 4, 2017, http://www.hpechildrenandyouth.ca/2013/08/what-does-no-wrong-door-and-warm-hand-off-really-mean/

5    Community Solutions, https://www.community.solutions

6    Sanjay Gupta, Tim Hume, and Ben Tinker, "'Our mouths were ajar:' Doctor's Fight to Expose Flint's Water Crisis," CNN, January 22, 2016, http://www.cnn.com/2016/01/21/health/flint-water-mona-hanna-attish/index.html

7    Peter Muennig, "The Social Costs of Lead Poisonings," *Health Affairs* 35, no. 8. 1545, August 2016, http://content.healthaffairs.org/content/35/8/1545.3.full

8    Mark Aalfs et al., "Indicators of Sustainable Communities," *Sustainable Seattle*, 1998, http://www.oecd.org/site/worldforum/33732840.pdf

9    "Air and Water Quality: Why Are Air and Water Quality Important to Health?" *County Health Rankings*, 2017, http://www.countyhealthrankings.org/our-approach/health-factors/air-water-quality

10    "Outdoor Air," National Center for Environmental Health, last modified September 8, 2017, https://ephtracking.cdc.gov/showAirHIA.action

11    Jennifer Wang, "The Health Impacts of Energy Choices," Health Energy Initiative, *Healthcare Without Harm*, October 2015.

12    Richard W. Clapp, "Nuclear Power and Public Health," *Environmental Health Perspective* 113, no. 11 A720–A721, November 2005.

13    Bruce Biewald, Jonathan J. Buonocore, Jeremy Fisher, Jonathan I. Levy, Patrick Luckow, Gregory Norris, John D. Spengler, "Health and Climate Benefits of Different Energy-Efficient and Renewable Energy Choices," *Nature Climate Change, August 31,* 2015.

14    Nick Watts et al., "Health and Climate Change Policy: Policy Responses to Protect Public Health," *The Lancet Commissions* 386, no. 10006, 1861–1914, November 7, 2015.

15    Sustainable Cities: Bloomberg Foundation, https://www.bloomberg.org/program/environment/sustainable-cities/#overview

16    P. J. Hamilton, M. G. Marmot, M. Shipley, and Geoffery Rose, "Employment Grade and Coronary Heart Disease in British Civil Servants," *Journal of Epidemiology and Community Health* 32, no. 4, 244–249, December 1978, https://www.ncbi.nlm.nih.gov/pmc/articles/PMC1060958/pdf/jepicomh200004-0017.pdf

17    "Reducing Health Disparities—Role of the Health Sector: Discussion Paper," Health Disparities Task Group of the Federal/Provincial/Territorial Advisory Committee on Population Health and Health Security, Public Health Agency Canada, Ottawa, December 2004, accessed March 31, 2017.

18    C. Barclay, P. Braveman, S. Egerter, "Income, Wealth, and Health," *Exploring the Social Determinants of Health*, no. 4, Robert Wood Johnson Foundation, April 2011, http://www.rwjf.org/en/library/research/2011/04/how-social-factors-shape-health1.html

19    Margot Sangor-Katz, "Income Inequality: It's Also Bad for Your Health," *The New York Time: TheUpshot*, March 30, 2015, https://www.nytimes.com/2015/03/31/upshot/income-inequality-its-also-bad-for-your-health.html?mcubz=3

20    Walker et al. "Effects of Psychosocial Stimulation and Dietary Supplementation n Early Childhood on Psychosocial Functioning in Late Adolescence: Follow-Up of Randomized Controlled Trial," *BMJ* 333, 472, August 31, 2006, accessed Mar 31 2017, https://doi.org/10.1136/bmj.38897.555208.2F

21    Mother Teresa, BrainyQuote, accessed August 16, 2017, https://www.brainyquote.com/quotes/quotes/m/mothertere130839.html

22    J.S. House, "Social Isolation Kills, But How and Why?" *Psychosomatic Medicine* 63, no. 2, 273-274, March/April 2001.

23    Robert Putnam, "Bowling Alone: The Collapse and Revival of American Community," *Simon & Schuster*, 2000.

24    Don Cohen, Lewis Feldstein, and Robert Putnam, "Better Together: Restoring the American Community," *Simon & Schuster*, 2003

25    Robert Putnam, "Going Bowling," interview by Robert Putnam, *All Things Considered*, NPR, May 31, 2000, audio, 7:30, accessed April 1, 2017.

# GATHER RESOURCES

**CHALLENGE:** Can we gather resources in our hometowns to address the social determinants of health?

## MYRICK TRADING POST—RESOURCES AVAILABLE FOR POPULATION HEALTH

Just to provide a bit of history and context about La Crosse. La Crosse is located at the convergence of three big rivers: Mississippi River, Black River, and La Crosse River. It is the largest city in western Wisconsin, and sits right along the Wisconsin–Minnesota boarder. Historically, there was a larger community—a trading post—established further downstream along the Mississippi River before settlers arrived in La Crosse. But a man named Nathan Myrick had the insight to set up a new trading post further upstream, right at the intersection of three key rivers, so that La Crosse would have a competitive advantage.

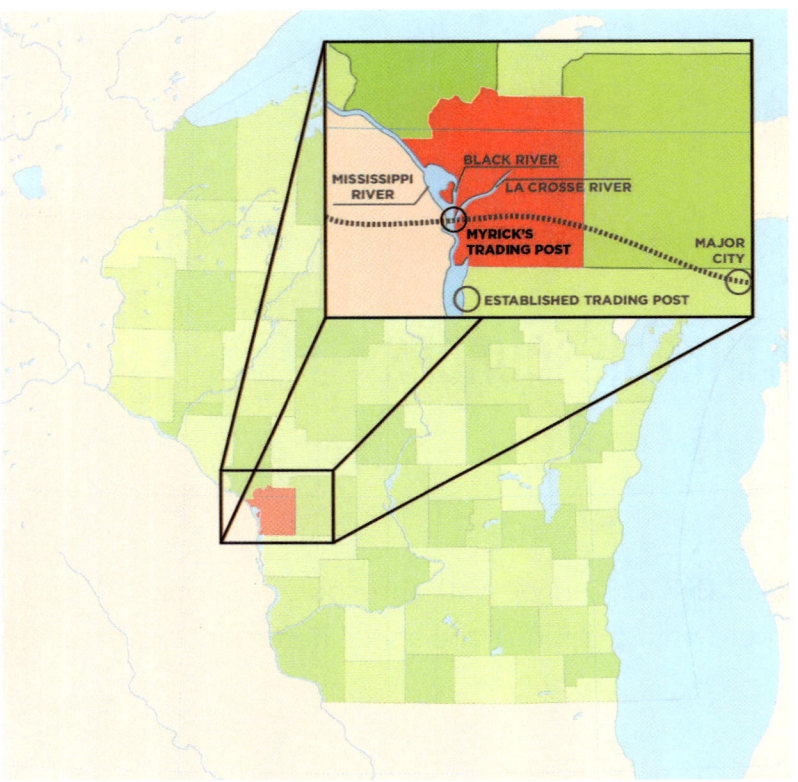

 **FIGURE 5.1. Move Upstream to Build a Thriving Community**

*The city of La Crosse was founded when a young entrepreneur, Nathan Myrick, decided to open a trading post upstream. The new trading post was closer to the work of fur trappers and easier to reach for traders travelling from Milwaukee to Minneapolis. The combination—close to work, accessible to finance—made La Crosse thrive despite the decline of fur trading and rise of multiple industries: timber, dairy, and manufacturing.*

In the 1840s, rivers were primary pathways for transportation. Goods and services were exchanged at river trading posts, driving the developing economy. Fur trappers would travel along the rivers, bringing goods to sell to the trading posts. Traders would come to trading posts to buy furs at lower prices. The most time-consuming, expensive, and rate-limiting factor in the developing fur economy was the trappers transporting furs. By moving further upstream— and closer to the trappers work—Myrick was able to cut down the amount of time trappers spent making the difficult trip against the current to collect furs, attract trappers from all three river basins, and accumulate a wider selection of furs for traders. In addition, La Crosse was midway between two of the largest cities in the developing Midwest—Chicago and Minneapolis. Traders would have the option of which market to connect with. Eventually, the biggest road—and only ford across the Mississippi—was built from Chicago to Minneapolis through La Crosse. Now traders could buy mercantile goods produced in Chicago, sell in Minneapolis, and pick up additional furs to bring to market in Minnesota. The traders could then purchase goods in Minneapolis, return through La Crosse, pick up more furs, and bring goods from both cities to sell in Chicago. The location of the trading post maximized efficiency by reducing the travel times of frontline workers. In addition, the connection between rivers and roads lowered barriers between producers and profitable markets. La Crosse became a center for more than just the fur trade—timber, cattle, dairy, farming, and even manufacture thrived at the intersection of three rivers. When it came time to build a railroad, policymakers decided to build through La Crosse. Now the city was tightly integrated through three different avenues—river, road, and rail—to the economy of the Midwest. The key to growth was creating connections between existing resources. La Crosse was able to grow, to expand, to adapt, and to thrive because Nathan Myrick located his trading post upstream, closer to the work, and then connected his community to a diverse set of funding streams.

Health may be determined by where you live, work, learn, and play. But the additional—and potentially transformational—insight is this: your community's resources are frequently concentrated right next to the neighborhoods with the greatest needs.

It is possible to draw a parallel between the historical development of La Crosse and the GRACE project. We endeavored to move upstream from the health system and address population health in communities at the intersection of multiple different funding streams: social capital, grants, private philanthropy, and public funding.

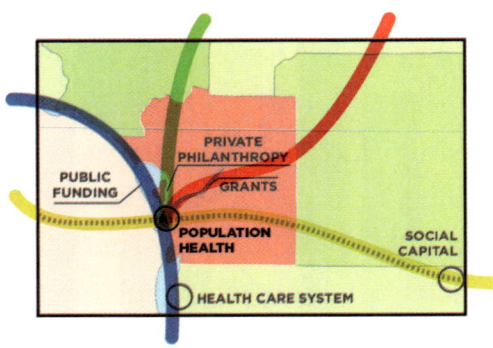

 **FIGURE 5.2. Population Health Is Upstream from Healthcare Systems**

*US healthcare systems are well funded but not necessarily positioned to directly impact the upstream drivers of health and disease. Clinical care cannot overcome the social, economic, and environmental forces that drive health outcomes. If we want to build healthy communities, then we need to pay for population at the intersection of public funding, private philanthropy, grants, and social capital. Healthy communities can be sustainably financed by healthcare dollars alone.*

The primary drivers of health were the social determinants, not the clinical care provided by the health system. It did not make sense to have healthcare providers working outside their area of expertise to address social needs. While clinics can be important resources for identifying unmet social needs, the funding and the services would be better utilized and more sustainably funded if we used existing community programs. We wanted to work at the intersection of public funding and private philanthropy. We wanted our grant-funded activities to connect with sustainable social capital and reliable business models. And we wanted healthcare to partner with social service agencies to support vulnerable families. The idea was to spread the risk of a new project across multiple funders and stakeholders, but maximize the access and opportunities to expand services for families living in key neighborhoods.

## GATHER RESOURCES

We need to gather resources if we want to transition from wasteful healthcare to wellness-focused population health. In the US, we have a spending problem. The combination of an underfunded public health and social service sector shifts the financial burden from community organizations to hospital systems. "[There is] an American tendency to funnel resources earmarked for health toward medical care," observed Bradley and Taylor. "These historical realities make clear that Americans have been complicit in the creation of the current approach." Another researcher, Steffie Woolhandler, who handled the public health expenditure in the US over the last fifty years, concluded, "Public health activities offer a broad range of health and financial benefits: a longer, healthier life, more productive workers for industry, lower anticipated Medicare and Medicaid spending, lower insurance premiums for everyone else, and children better able to focus on their education and grow into healthy adults."[2] Yet we keep funneling money into medical care, instead of public health, population health, and prevention services.

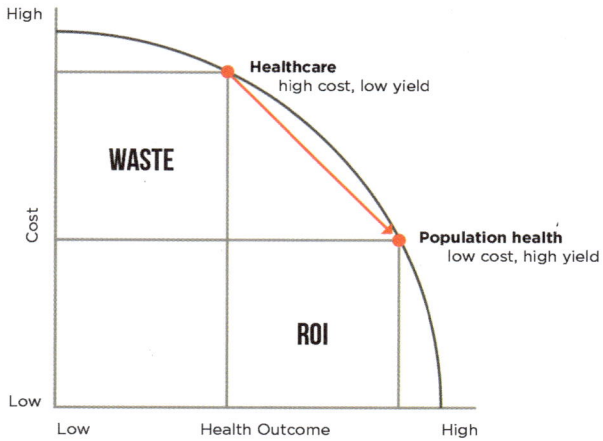

**FIGURE 5.3. Gather Resources to Transition from Healthcare to Population Health**

Communities need local, unrestricted funds to finance population health priorities. Healthcare is expensive and healthcare systems determine less than one fifth of overall health outcomes. Population health programs cost one tenth as much as healthcare but produce longer-term improvements in health outcomes. The transition from expensive healthcare system to healthy communities can begin when communities gather resources to prioritize population health.

We can break the cycle of under-investment in better health outcomes by clearly connecting social data to medical outcomes. If we can show stakeholders how much the status quo costs and how little health their money is buying, then we can make progress toward reforming reimbursement.

The transition from expensive healthcare to effective population health will require community stakeholders to invest in population health programs and infrastructure. If we can gather resources by identifying and reducing healthcare waste, then even if only a fraction of the cost-savings can be invested in community efforts, there will be enough funds to pay for population health. The result is a win–win. Healthcare payers save money; population health providers have new opportunities for sustainable financing. When we looked at how much current groups were paying and the opportunities for saving in a county with a hundred thousand people, the leadership was amazed. How will we pay for addressing population health? A good start is to address waste and lost revenue for stakeholders by going upstream and addressing the root causes of social and medical spending. Prevention costs money, but it is so much cheaper than crisis care and responding to emergencies.

City and county administrators, healthcare and insurance executives, as well as business leaders who are willing to invest 10 percent of their community savings annually in evidence-based population health collaborations will see significant financial windfall. Leaders are tired of charity that doesn't help. There is a desire for social investing and the algorithms to connect dollars spent on addressing the social determinants of health with community savings. We will pay for population health by encouraging local leaders to invest in the health and well-being of the community.

The challenge is not just who will pay, but also how to ensure the community money is well spent. Current systems and structures for funding population health are broken. The financing is short-term and disconnected from community outcomes. Money flows downward from payers to issue-based programs, and limited information about results or community outcomes is available. There is significant redundancy because financing comes with strings—additional program requirements, reporting expectations, and lots of back office issues. The provider agencies are constantly restructuring their organizations to qualify for new funding opportunities. There is no opportunity for collective impact reporting, shared overhead, or collaboration across issue-based programs.

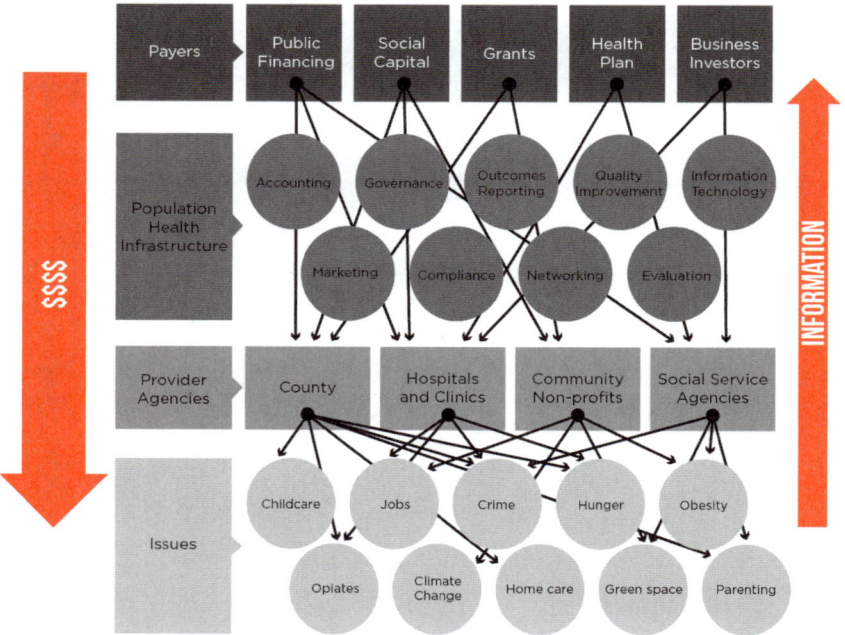

**FIGURE 5.4. Current Broken System for Financing Population Health**

*Our current system of paying for population health programs depends on payers funding pilots by providers' agencies to address specific issues. For each issue in the community, local county agencies, clinics, community nonprofits, and social service agencies compete for funding from external payers. Payers often place intensive reporting requirements on provider agencies to ensure that funds are well spent. However, the system results in redundant population health infrastructure that cannot be shared and does not respond quickly to evolving community threats or opportunities for collaboration. The broken system fails to provide information to payers on return on investment or social impact. In the end, the current system handicaps provider agencies, frustrates payers, and fails to effectively address the issues that impact health and well-being of families.*

The downside is that the first $100,000 of every new initiative gets diverted to cover infrastructure costs—the back office tasks necessary for good governance, data collection, and accountability and program evaluation. Most respectable funders—whether it be state government, foundations, or other grant makers—require some version of outcomes reporting. [There are limits on how funds can be used, where and for whom money can be spent, and strict requirements for reporting.] When every project has a different funder, the reality is that one organization—such as the county health department—may have five or six different reports due at any one time. The result is that staff are pulled from serving in a direct care capacity and repurposed to servicing payer demands.

In La Crosse, we wanted to make the system more rational. We wanted to see funding flow to organizations that had existing programs with sufficient workforce to address the primary needs in the community. Rather than building new programs for every problem, we wanted the infrastructure to be flexible enough to address a range of issues—health behaviors, clinical care, social and economic factors, and physical environment—without requiring additional overhead. The ideal was to have one independent, neutral agent that would shoulder the back office burden—accounting, reporting, information technology, evaluation, compliance, and governance—while releasing more funds with fewer restrictions to provider agencies. The neutral agent would be able to aggregate results from multiple different agencies and report to funders on both collective community impact and key unmet needs that might be addressed through new investment.

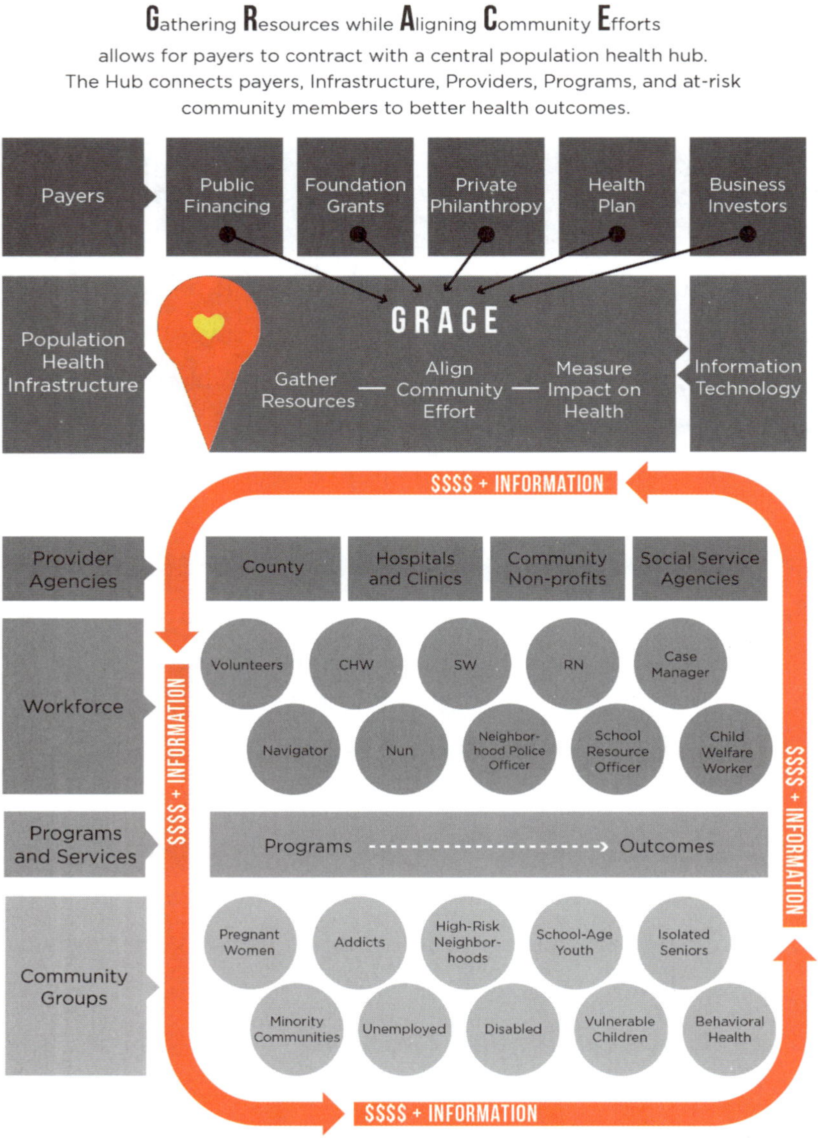

Gathering Resources while Aligning Community Efforts
allows for payers to contract with a central population health hub.
The Hub connects payers, Infrastructure, Providers, Programs, and at-risk
community members to better health outcomes.

## FIGURE 5.5. Gather Resources to Improve Population Health

*There are many strategies to gather resources for population health priorities. This is the strategy behind backbone organizations, anchor missions, accountable health communities, and pathways community hubs. The key is to keep money local, connect payments to community outcomes, and improve coordination between community agencies. The result—collective impact—means improving population health outcomes for families.*

It is important to connect payments, programs, people, and population health outcomes. An additional benefit was that provider agencies can focus on building up their workforce and achieving their mission, instead of constantly chancing grant funding. Successful programs—the projects that improved health outcomes for families—would be rewarded for being effective, not just novel. By gathering resources at a hub—in La Crosse, the hub shares staff between United Way and the county health department—and utilizing existing staff at high-performing community organizations, we can better align population health priorities and affect just and lasting community transformation.

We recognize that results must be measured at the household level. It is not enough to report community averages. We wanted better data to drive policymaking and future investments. By connecting social factors to medical outcomes, we will be able to make concrete statements about population health—including quality of life, length of life, and costs to the community.

The GRACE (Gathering Resources Aligning Community Engagement) Hub accelerates collaboration, reducing the incentives for individual community organizations to vertically integrate social programs. Instead of competing with each other for funding, county health, hospitals and clinics, community nonprofits, and social services agencies collaborate with each other. The organizations can benefit from the shared information technology platform and financing options provided through the hub. The hub, not the individual organizations, can report to funds and provide infrastructure to support good governance, accountability, transparency, and performance evaluation. What is more, the hub helps to disseminate best practices across community organizations.

## Why Might Healthcare Be the Wrong System to Lead Population Health Initiatives?

I do not think that healthcare systems should be the hub for population health, for these reasons:

- Healthcare systems manage resources inefficiently.

- Healthcare organizations frequently compete against one another within a geographic community—such as a neighborhood, city, or county—leading to a potential conflict of interest between market share and community well-being.

- Community organizations fear that healthcare leaders will "medicalize" population health strategies.

- Healthcare systems face internal divisions over issues of mission, mission creep, scope of service, and how best to empower patients.

We are talking about differences in orders of magnitude between healthcare systems and county health departments. Social service providers and community nonprofits are financially farther downstream from money than healthcare systems and county health departments are, leading to competition for financial scraps in the form of community benefit dollars, grants, and partnerships with the "big" players—healthcare systems, foundations and government agencies. In addition:

- Healthcare systems are often too big and too geographically spread out to work at a local level to address the social needs of patients.

- Healthcare systems have a reputation for being fickle community partners. Population health success requires years and possibly even decades of focused, disciplined progress in a single strategic direction.

- Healthcare systems have been slow to shift their payment models upstream to connect with public health, philanthropy, and social services. Why? Healthcare in the US is hugely profitable.

Healthcare systems—as opposed to county health departments, social service providers, and nonprofit organizations—have all the money. When you think about integrated healthcare systems, you are thinking about billion and multi-billion dollar organizations that serve a number of communities. County health departments have budgets of millions and are focused on a discrete geographic area. Social service organizations have budgets in the hundreds of thousands, whereas community nonprofit organizations have budgets in tens of thousands.

Healthcare systems don't know what their role and responsibility is to population health. Sometimes, population health is described as something that occurs outside of healthcare delivery, such as a community's rates of obesity, crime, or high school graduation. More often, population health management or population medicine is viewed as clinical interventions aimed at specific patient subsets (e.g., high-need, high-cost patients), with the overall goal of improving care delivery (e.g., reducing readmissions) and reducing costs. The time is right for a paradigm shift. We are finally at a moment in the history when we know what to do to achieve better health, who should do it, and how to get it done.

## GATHERING RESOURCES CAN LEAD TO UPSTREAM FINANCING FOR POPULATION HEALTH

There is a strong financial case to be made for communities investing cash in population health programs. Early investments from local stakeholders can provide much-needed capital to under-resourced communities. It can help distribute risk across multiple stakeholders. It fosters ownership, as local leaders now have "skin in the game." Depending on the risk tolerance of stakeholders and willingness to experiment with financing vehicles, population health can be financed by a variety of mechanisms.

The upstream, local financing makes it easier to negotiate contracts with large payers, such as insurance providers, government, foundations, and the healthcare system. These are the main stakeholders financing health in our counties. The health plans and local government have the greatest financial risk if community resources are poorly allocated away from effective interventions. But they are not capable of contracting with forty-plus different provider organizations. It is much easier for payers to link upstream financing to a desired community or medical outcome, then let a hub manage the implementation, dissemination and collective impact reporting. When population health improves and costs to the community begin to fall, the upstream financing mechanisms can document and "capture" savings to payers and encourage payers to reinvest a portion of the savings in efficient, effective programs. Thus, a virtuous cycle of: invest-save-capture-reinvest.

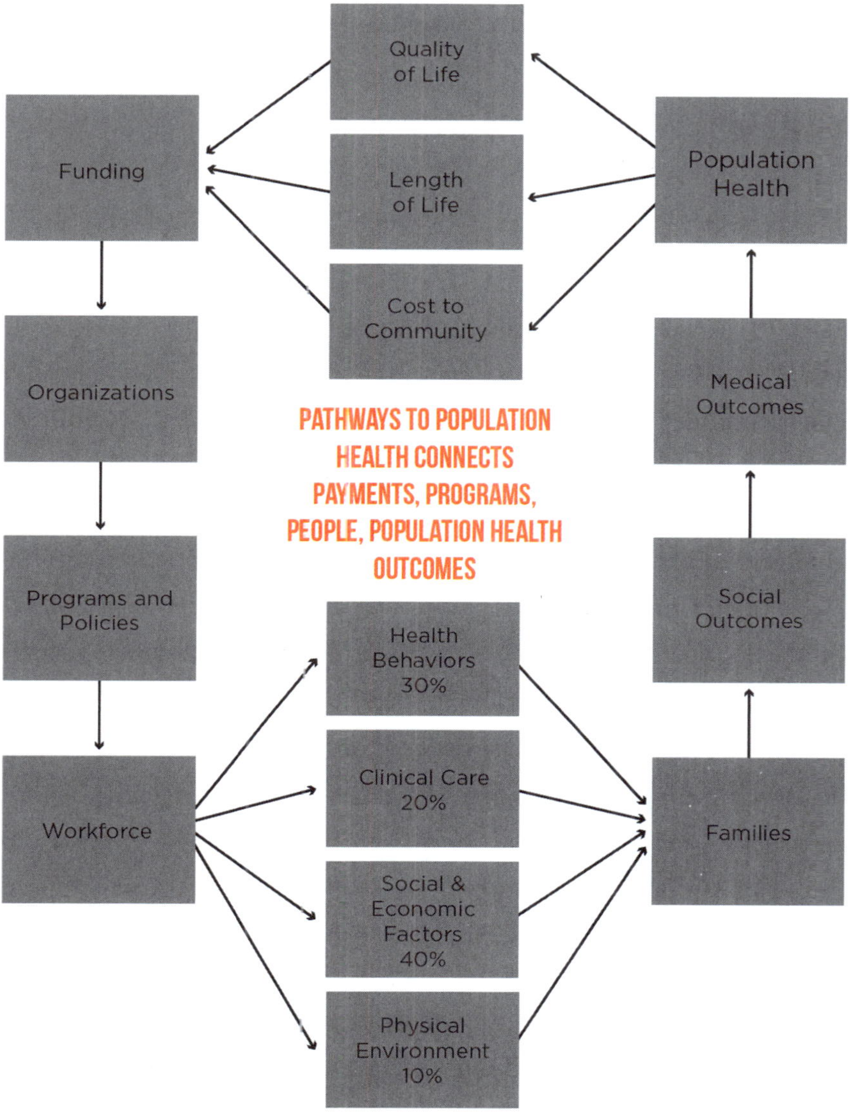
Quality of Life
Funding
Length of Life
Population Health
Cost to Community
Organizations
Medical Outcomes
PATHWAYS TO POPULATION HEALTH CONNECTS PAYMENTS, PROGRAMS, PEOPLE, POPULATION HEALTH OUTCOMES
Programs and Policies
Social Outcomes
Health Behaviors 30%
Workforce
Clinical Care 20%
Families
Social & Economic Factors 40%
Physical Environment 10%

**FIGURE 5.6. Paying for Population Health**

*The transition from pilot funding to paying for population health at scale in US communities will not be easy. In healthcare, progress toward value-based payments has been made when success is dependent on identifiable actors with the resources to change processes and influence outcomes. Paying for population health is more complicated because the goals are broad and there is no single fiduciary for a community good. We need to follow the money from payments to programs to people to population health outcomes.*

I believe that it is vital to connect payments, programs, people, and population health outcomes. An additional benefit was that organizations will be able to focus on building up their workforce and achieving their mission, instead of constantly chancing grant funding. Successful programs—the projects that improved health outcomes for families—would be rewarded for being effective, not just novel.

## CHALLENGES TO GATHERING RESOURCES

### Four Key Barriers to Sustainability

There are four systemic problems that prevent sustainable population health funding at the local level. The four problems are:

1. Population health programs tend to operate in silos, instead of bridging across sectors

2. Population health programs chase grant funding to pay for operation expenses

3. Population health programs are burdened by the excessive regulations present in healthcare, public health, and social service sectors.

4. Population health programs tend to emphasize prevention, which pays less than crisis care.

It is possible to gather resources when we address payment reform and provide clear mechanisms to help stakeholders change their business models.

## Problem #1—Programs Operating in Silos

The 1988 Institute of Medicine Report, *The Future of Public Health*, called for broad, crosscutting skills and competencies for public health practitioners. In 2014, researchers convened a national leadership consisting representing thirty-one different professional associations in healthcare and public health.[3] The representatives were asked to look beyond their discipline-specific priorities and collectively assess the priorities, needs, and characteristics of the workforce needed to improve the health and well-being of the entire community. The highest priority skills were:

- systems thinking

- communicating persuasively

- change management/adaptability/flexibility

The researchers went on to point out the benefits of bringing key workforce partners together and holding them accountable for improving community outcomes. The combination of systems experts, communicating persuasively, and managing change together for the benefit of the community will help overcome the silos in healthcare, public health, social services, and community nonprofits. The researchers conclude:

> *[Population] health is silo-driven without a unified, consistent identity. Instead of a unified position, competition among public health specialty areas such as chronic disease or emergency preparedness (i.e., the "silos") for legislative and public attention and categorical funding has nurtured silos rather than addressed the crosscutting needs common to all [population] health workers.*[4]

The added benefit of community-based collaboration is the possibility of aligning financial incentives with population health outcomes.

## Problem #2—Chasing Grants to Pay Operational Expenses

Budget shortfalls have resulted in extensive staffing shortages at local, state, and federal levels. These seriously challenge the ability of community stakeholders to leverage the opportunities for improved population health. To fully maximize population health opportunities, community providers should share resources between programs. The result is lower overhead on a per-program basis, and great community capacity to adapt new opportunities. However, program-specific funding regulations directly inhibit development of program "agnostic," multiuse infrastructure. In an article title "Creating Value," author, researcher, and informaticist Arthur Davidson argues:

> *Architects do not design separate plumbing systems for each room in a house; one hot water heater serves the entire building. Similarly, a PH agency should be able to share technologies and gain efficiencies across program areas. Technologies are ever-changing; PH departments need to strategically manage their technology portfolio to assure reasonable upfront and depreciated costs and investment return. By designing and building for aligned, cross-program, and cross-department functionality, PH agencies can encourage technology reuse, make more affordable investments, lower total cost of operations, and improve investment return.*[5]

There is a frustrating, persistent myth that public health and social services are inefficient. It is not true. In the *Nonprofit Overhead Cost Study*, a five-year research project conducted by the Urban Institute's National Center for Charitable Statistics and the Center on Philanthropy at Indiana University, researchers examined more than 220,000 IRS Form 990s and conducted 1,500 in-depth surveys of organizations with revenues of more than $100,000.

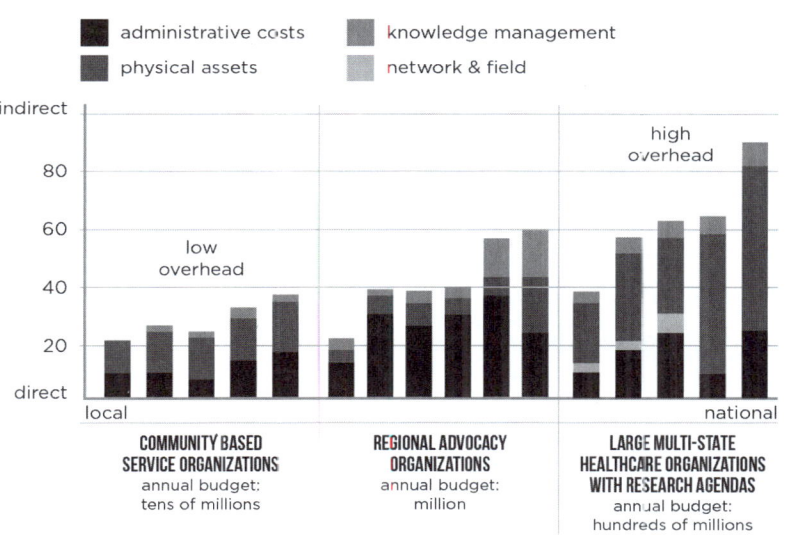

 **FIGURE 5.7. Comparing Overhead between Direct Service Organizations and Research Organizations**[6]

*Unfortunately, community-based direct service organizations tend to underinvest in learning networks and knowledge management. Large healthcare organizations with research agendas tend to have higher indirect-to-direct costs but also receive three to four times as much funding as direct service organizations. If we can gather resources and connect the strengths of direct service organizations with the funding, learning*

*networks, and knowledge management skills of research organizations, then we will be able to prioritize and pay for population health.*

Direct service providers, in fields such as public health and social services, were some of the lowest-overhead, most-efficient organizations that researchers analyzed. When key stakeholders at these nonprofits were asked about the barriers that prevented a transition from dependency on grant funding toward self-sufficiency through value-based payments, stakeholders acknowledged the roles of funders, workers, and leadership:

- funder inflexibility leading to staff feeling frustrated

- time constraints on workers caused by increased workloads and burnout

- dwindling support from leaders as positions and programs are cut[7]

Appropriate funding for operational expenses allows organizations to invest in learning networks, effective technology, and staff training. When it is the outcome—not specific activity—that is rewarded, community organizations are freed to innovate.

## Problem #3—Excessive Regulation

Not all regulation is bad. "[Public Health] Law can be empowering," writes Lawrence Gostin. He continues:

*Of the 10 great public health achievements of the 20th century, most were realized, at least in part, through law reform or litigation: vaccinations, safer workplaces, safer and healthier foods, motor vehicle safety, control of infectious diseases, tobacco control, and fluoridation of drinking water.[8]*

The problem is that many well-intended regulations intended to protect individual rights inhibit organizations from collaborating, due to fear of litigation or regulatory penalties. It is expensive to comply the dizzying array of local, state, and federal regulations that govern population health. "In order to navigate safely," notes Villalobos, "population health organizations must rely upon in-house counsel, external counsel, IT experts, compliance officers, privacy and security officers, and consultants galore."[9] Most small community collaboration do not have the technical or legal resources to think through all the implication of a cross-sector community collaboration.

Consider the regulations—local, regional, state, and federal—that limit a healthcare system. Gundersen Health System diagrammed all of the compliance requirements on an integrated health system in Wisconsin.

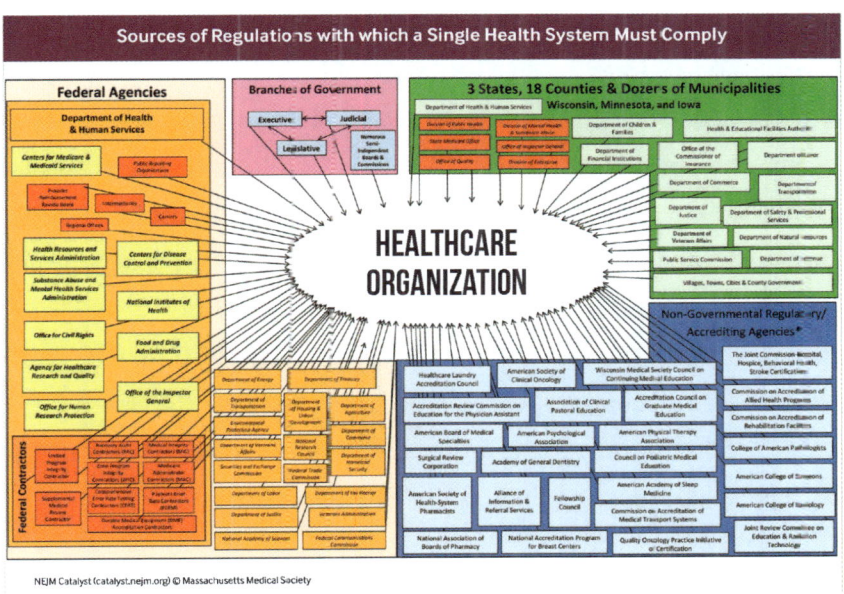

NEJM Catalyst (catalyst.nejm.org) © Massachusetts Medical Society

**FIGURE 5.8. Sources of Regulation For Healthcare Systems**

*Kari Adank, Gundersen Health System's chief compliance officer, and Jeff Thompson, Gundersen Health System's CEO, designed an infographic to help explain the cost of compliance with regulations. Every healthcare system will have a somewhat different set of regulators, but the volume and lack of coordination across governing bodies and agencies consistently results in conflicting laws, inefficiency, and a focus on the rules, taking attention away from the well-being of patients and communities. Source: NEJM Catalyst*

Jeff Thompson, whom I mentioned earlier as a leader who taught me about the Culture of Health, developed this figure to illustrate the dizzying complexity of healthcare regulation. He says:

> *Although the U.S. Constitution does not mention health, over the last 200 years healthcare's vital role has resulted in thousands of federal, state, local, and non-governmental rules from well-intentioned lawmakers and regulators who are trying to improve on a complex system.*[10]

All of these sources of regulation represent a minefield for potential collaborations. In addition, the nature of in-the-trenches population health—iconoclastic, grassroots, get-good-done under-the-radar—means your best plans may be foiled by a midlevel managers, nurse administrator, Nervous-Nellie doctor-turned-vice president, lawyer from risk management, or municipal drone hell-bent on opposing any new-fangled changes—good, bad, or indifferent.

But there is help. The Network for Public Health Law exists to provide information and technical assistance on issues related to public health, population health, and community collaboration. The legal advice is free, and the lawyers have expertise in:

- drug overdose prevention

- environmental public health

- health reform

- health information and data sharing

- maternal and child health

- public health statues and regulatory information

I routinely use and reference the expert webinars, policy briefs, and research articles distributed by the Network of Public Health Law.[11] They are a fantastic group, and actively work to improve the health and well-being of communities across the US through advocacy and legal reform.

## Problem #4—The Wrong Financial Incentives

Paul B. Ginsburg, from the University of Southern California's Schaeffer Center for Health Policy and Economics, argues in the *Wall Street Journal* that "fee for service," the default strategy for funding healthcare in the US, "makes little sense."[12] Multiple physician advocacy groups have called for payment reform. Michael Porter, the Harvard Business School guru who helped Paul Farmer create the Global Health Delivery course, says, "The fee-for-service system, the dominant payment model in the U.S. and many other countries, is now widely recognized as perhaps the single biggest obstacle to improving healthcare delivery."[13]

The Patient Protection and Affordable Care Act (ACA)— popularly known as Obamacare—promised to ensure better access to healthcare for many Americans through expanded public and private insurance coverage, including basic preventive healthcare. This was an attempt to pay for prevention. The ACA had four financial incentives that, if implemented, would improve population health at the local level:

1. Community Health Assessments and Community Health Implementation Plans

2. Linking clinical and community prevention to outcome-based payments

3. Supporting alternative payment methodologies to pay for prevention, like value-based payments, accountable care organizations, and accountable health communities

4. Providing incentives for coordination of care and building the nontraditional health workforce, such as health navigators and community health workers

Jean O'Connor, JD MPH, and Melvin Kohn, MD MPH, have worked for years as public health directors. When reflecting on the potential for payment reform to improve population health, they note:

> Public health can play a key role in this transformation to ensure that people and communities have the tools to be healthy for decades to come. To do this, public health and public and private payers must collaborate to measure the health of the population, knit together reinforcing systems of community and clinical prevention, pay for approaches that create healthy communities, and build upon existing community resources for care coordination and develop the community health workforce.[14]

Michel Porter argues:

> The time has come to change the way we pay for healthcare, in the United States and around the world. It [our payment method] entrenches large existing systems, eliminates patient choice, promotes more consolidation, limits competition, and perpetuates the lack of provider accountability for outcomes. It will fail again to drive true innovation in healthcare delivery.[15]

Population health improves when we provide evidence-based interventions that address the root causes of health and disease. Benjamin Franklin said, "An ounce of preventions is worth a pound of cure." We need to break the incentive structures that reward crisis control instead of crisis prevention.

## REFLECTION QUESTIONS

1. Take a population health program that you are familiar with. Did multiple community stakeholders participate in the program? How was the fit between organizations? How did the organizations respect, or fail to respect, each other's contributions?

2. Peter Drucker is famous for the adage: "It is not enough for a business to do well; it must also do good. But in order to do good, a business must first do well." Now think about a population health effort in your community. How well was it executed?

3. Think about payers, population health infrastructure, provider agencies, programs, workforce, and populations. Where are the opportunities in your community to accelerate systems change? Who would be willing to help you?

---

**PART 5 ENDNOTES**

1   Elizabeth Bradley and Lauren Taylor, "The American Healthcare Paradox," *Public Affairs*, 2013.
2   Lisa Rapaport, "U.S. Public Health Funding on the Decline," *Reuters*, November 18, 2015, http://www.reuters.com/article/us-health-publichealth-funding-idUSKCN0T735R20151118

3   "The Future of Public Health," Committee for the Study of the Future of Public Health Division of Health Care Services Institute of Medicine, *National Academy Press*, 1988, https://www.nap.edu/read/1091

4   N.J. Kaufman et al., "Thinking Beyond the Silos: Emerging Priorities in Workforce Development for State and Local Government Public Health Agencies," *Journal of Public Health Management and Practice* 20, no. 6, 557-565, November/December 2014.

5   Arthur J. Davidson, "Creating Value: Unifying Silos into Public Health Business Intelligence," *The Journal for Electronic Health Data and Methods* 2, no. 4, March 30, 2015, https://www.ncbi.nlm.nih.gov/pmc/articles/PMC4438104/

6   Jeri Eckhart-Queenan, Michael Etzel, and Sridhar Prasad. "Pay-What-Takes Philanthropy" *Sanford Social Innovation Review*. Summer 2016.

7   Ann Goggins Gregory and Don Howard, "The Nonprofit Starvation Cycle," *Stanford Social Innovation Review*, 2009, https://ssir.org/articles/entry/the_nonprofit_starvation_cycle

8   Lawrence Gostin, "Law and the Public's Health," *Issues in Science and Technology* 21, no. 3, 2005, http://issues.org/21-3/gostin/

9   Keith Loria, "The Regulatory Challenges of Population Health," *For the Record* 29, no. 1, 18, Jan 2017, http://www.fortherecordmag.com/archives/0117p18.shtml

10  Jeff Thompson, "My Favorite Slide: Sources of Regulation with Which a Single Health System Must Comply," *NEJM Catalyst*, April 21, 2016, http://catalyst.nejm.org/my-favorite-slide-sources-of-regulations-with-which-a-single-health-system-must-comply/

11  The Network for Public Health Law, https://www.networkforphl.org

12  Paul Ginsburg, "Should the U.S. Move Away from Fee-For-Service Medicine?" *The Wall Street Journal,* May 2015, https://www.wsj.com/articles/should-the-u-s-move-away-from-fee-for-service-medicine-1427079653

13  Robert Kaplan and Michael Porter, "How to Pay for Healthcare," *Harvard Business Review*, July/August 2016, https://hbr.org/2016/07/how-to-pay-for-health-care

14  Jean O'Connor et al., "Paying for Prevention: A Critical Opportunity for Public Health," *The Journal of Law Medicine and Ethics* 41, no. 1, 69-72, March 2013.

15  Robert Kaplan and Michael Porter, "How to Pay for Healthcare," *Harvard Business Review*, July/August 2016, https://hbr.org/2016/07/how-to-pay-for-health-care

PART 6

# ALIGN COMMUNITY EFFORT

**CHALLENGE:** What can I do with $5K to improve population health?

Health Leads USA—a Boston-based nonprofit that helps healthcare systems design programs to screen, identify, and address patients' unmet social needs—has committed time, thought, and effort to clarify a *Shared Vision for Social Needs Programs.*[1] They spent six months convening expert panels representing population health leaders from the West Coast, Midwest, and the East Coast to answer the question: "What does good look like?" They came up with a proposal for a roadmap for population health that addresses unmet social needs.

I participated in this process. It was thoughtful, collaborative, and comprehensive. This framework was facilitated by Health Leads, supported by the Commonwealth Fund, and collaboratively produced by forty healthcare leaders, representing twenty-two healthcare institutions, in summer and fall 2016.

I have adapted the final document to help articulate what aligning community effort might look like in practice. The key is that you will be able to address, across a number of different core dimensions, how your organization connects to community efforts and how the community resources are aligned to the pressing unmet needs of families.

Aligning community effort helps communities: (1) define success from both the community perspective and the family's perspective; (2) tailor success by both degree and domain to allow for growth, change, and improvement; and (3) allow for a range of success to help communities track progress.

A range of responses to social need interventions may be meaningful for the family and the community. Defining levels of success to capture that range will enable more-nuanced understanding and improvements of interventions over time. It will be important for your partners to see progress early. The ability to state concrete goals, such as our community will address five of the nine foundational domains goal within six months, can help to mobilize support and engage partners.

Aligning community effort helps you identify the foundational attributes of a functioning population health system. Not every community will have the foundational attributes covered. In some places, it will take concerted effort to build the strong foundation. However, the foundation will help you to identify "We are here," the starting point. Then you will be able to track your progress as a community toward a better, healthier, aspirational state.

The aspiration attributes describe a community where resources align with needs to improve population health. The aspirational community has clearly defined routes to health. No matter what the variety of unmet needs are—medical, social, environmental, or economic—the community that Gathers Resources and Aligns Community Effort is the community that best empowers families to thrive where they live, work, learn, and play.

## ALIGN COMMUNITY EFFORTS: FROM FOUNDATIONAL TO ASPIRATIONAL

| | DOMAIN | STARTING POINT: FOUNDATION | FINAL GOAL: ASPIRATION |
|---|---|---|---|
| **IMPLEMENTATION** | **GEOGRAPHIC** | Neighborhood coordinated on common network. | All essential services are coordinated on a state-wide network. |
| | **PRIORITY POPULATION** | Families, especially parents with children, veterans, and working poor. | All community members have unmet basic needs proactively addressed. |
| | **IDENTIFICATION AND SCREENING** | The community has a clear understanding of the population at risk and a well-defined goal for addressing basic needs. | All actionable basic needs are identified using a variety of data sources and shared across partnering service organizations. |
| | **NAVIGATION AND RESOURCE CONNECTIONS** | The community routinely completes a resource/needs assessment to match basic needs with appropriate services. | Community workers help families address needs quickly and efficiently all basic needs are referred, tracked and addressed. |
| | **TEAM AND WORKFLOW** | The community has workflows and processes to determine where and how to screen, refer and navigate resources. | All members of the community team collaborate to improve the social, medical, and behavioral factors driving health. |
| **DELIVERY** | **DATA AND EVALUATION** | The community articulates a theory of change, defines measures of success, and ensures reliable data collection. | The community undertakes sophisticated outcomes and evaluations that demonstrate the collective impact of community programs. |
| | **COMMUNITY PARTNERSHIPS** | The community has a sound base of knowledge of the resources available and has established relationships with key resource providers. | Public Health, Health Care, and Non-profit organizations align efforts around a common mission to achieve shared value for population health. |
| | **LEADERSHIP** | The community members have an active voice in assessing readiness for change at all levels. The community has established an appropriate change management strategy. | All sectors of the community embrace their role in addressing the basic needs of families. Community organizations collaborate to sustain improvements in population health. |
| | **FINANCING** | The community has a benchmark for current population health spending and costs to key stakeholders. | All sectors measure, capture and reinvest savings into sustainable population health improvements. Share value of population health is recognized by all stakeholders. |

**TABLE 6.1. Aligning Community Effort: From Foundational to Aspirational**

There are many challenges to aligning community effort. It will be important to consider the impact of population health on both smart implementation (including geography, priority population, identification and screening, navigation and resource connection, team, and workflow) and good governance (data and evaluation, community partnerships, leadership, and financing).

## ALIGNING COMMUNITY EFFORT ENABLES EFFECTIVE POPULATION HEALTH

Addressing the complexities of population health is beyond the scope of any one organization. To build the trust needed to advance health equity, and develop multi-sector partnerships and relationships with communities affected by health inequities, communities need to continually track results and improve efforts to maximize impact. Also, an aligned community effort will help identify cracks in the system, as well as the reasons why some families or organizations are not benefiting from the population health improvements.

Aligning community effort can help answer the question: what will community collaboration look like? By working through all nine domains as a community effort, there are four additional benefits that will help every community organization maximize performance.

## ALIGNING COMMUNITY EFFORT WILL PROVIDE FOUR CONCRETE ADVANTAGES

### Community Benefit #1—Collective Impact Reporting

**Collective Impact Reporting**—Hold staff accountable for these activities in training or performance plans. These expectations may help shift the culture and clarify everyone's role in advancing health equity. Addressing the complexities of health inequities is beyond the scope of any one organization or entity. To build the trust needed to advance health equity, develop multisector partnerships and relationships with communities affected by health inequities.

## Community Benefit #2—Reduced Overhead

**Improve Existing Programs by Sharing Costs**—A clear, shared population health strategy can help organizations reduce overhead. Human resources, marketing, purchasing, and reporting can be centralized to reap the benefits of economies of scale. Common policies can make it easier to get feedback from community members to ensure that services and resources are culturally and linguistically appropriate. In addition, sharing back office functions between organizations can ensure anticipated improvements are shared with community members to reinforce partnerships and relationships. The shared overhead makes community organizations leaner and more service focused, pleasing leaders, foundations, funders, and investors. But most importantly, shared operating expenses make informal collaborations on related initiatives much, much easier.

## Community Benefit #3— More Money to Address Social Determinants of Health

**Adequately Fund Programs when Stakeholders Recognized Shared Value**—Once a community has aligned effort, it will be easier to allocate funding to effective programs. Community service organizations will benefit from more community dollars allocated to successful programs. The criteria for funding will be clear, which promotes transparent processes for seeking, distributing, and using resources. It will also highlight unmet community needs and direct community agencies seeking resources toward population health priorities. This will ensure the most efficient use of time and money. Before funds are distributed, the aligning community effort framework will make population health a clear component of funding expectations and requirements to guide the actions of those receiving the funds (e.g., require hiring and collaborating with representatives from underserved communities, develop criteria for prioritizing interventions based on need).

## Community Benefit #4— Local Capacity to Respond to New and Emerging Population Health Problems

**Building Capacity**—I like to describe community capacity in terms of three types of workers. Imagine there were three workers, and each worker was given a set number of Ts. Time, Talent, Treasure, and Technology are all limited resources. In the story, the first two workers take risks, work hard, and achieve success. They are rewarded with more Ts. However, the third worker hoard his Ts. He takes no risks, does not do any work, and manages to do nothing. The third worker is penalized. All his Ts are given to the first worker, who had the most success. The moral of story, we are told:

> *To those who use well what they are given, even more will be given, and they will have an abundance. But from those who do nothing, even what little they have will be taken away. (Matthew 25:29, New Living Translation)*

Information technology, data science, and cloud computing can allow population health to scale rapidly. Rather than buying a new tool for every task, it will be important for communities to make smart decisions about when, where, and how to use technology to drive progress. Many US communities need a technological infrastructure to support referrals for unmet social needs. The task facing population health innovators is to help community organizations to collaborate with community partners and navigate the transition from competing organizations to a comprehensive, community-support system that will enhance the health and well-being of our patients, their families, our employees, and our community partners. It is important to recognize that tackling the community systems for screening, identification, and referral, and tracking for population health-related basic needs is a major project. In fact, most communities will have five or six different IT systems to help track and manage clients.

> **Current State**: There are five competing systems for population health, including health records, client databases, county health departments, and community nonprofits, to report activities and outcomes

> **Leading Change**: Motivated, frontline workers collaborate to fix a ridiculous situation and create one universal standard that covers everyone's (healthcare, public health, social services, payers, and business) cases.

> **Future State**: There are six competing systems.

Obviously, it is difficult to align community effort. But there are some common first steps that individuals can take to improve alignment.

## BUILD NETWORKS TO ADDRESS SDH

Build networks—formal and informal—in your community that can help to align community effort. Gathering Resources is a bottom-up activity; but aligning community effort requires buy-in from the top brass. The key to successfully aligning effort is to take advantage of existing programs, services, resources, and skills. If you can catch the interest of local leadership through small success and quick wins, then you may find yourself with opportunities to inspire action through shared visions and motivate collaboration on population health priorities.

## FOCUS ON WHAT WORKS FOR SDH

Focusing on what works can help you to choose effective programs and policies that promote learning networks and support the community workers within existing programs to have an impact. This will help avoid burnout and enhance community ownership—you will see how community ownership helps you act on what's important. In addition, community member participation will be important to achieving true quality for population health. With four-fifths of our community's health problems lying beyond the reach of a healthcare system or in the gaps between healthcare, public health, and social service, the answer cannot be incremental changes that ignore the root cause of the problem.

The World Health Organization has published a framework for how to tackle the SDH. The Infant Mortality Collaborative Improvement and Innovation Network (IM CoIIN) employed quality improvement, innovation, and collaborative learning to reduce infant mortality and improve birth outcomes. CoIIN focused on how communities can address SDH through: engaging leadership, fostering partnerships, building on existing programs, augmenting local capacity, and implementing evidence-based initiatives. Public and private leaders worked together building the infrastructure to work long term on policy and program approaches to shift the community focus to SDH and ensure health equity for women, infants, and families. IM CoIIN tested the process in nineteen states over three years. Most communities spent a small amount of money and focused on one or two upstream drivers of infant mortality. The results were significant improvements in babies surviving until their first birthday.

# TACKLING SOCIAL DETERMINANTS OF HEALTH USING EXISTING PROGRAMS

States in SDOH Learning Network and Strategy Selections, Phases 1 & 2, 2015-17

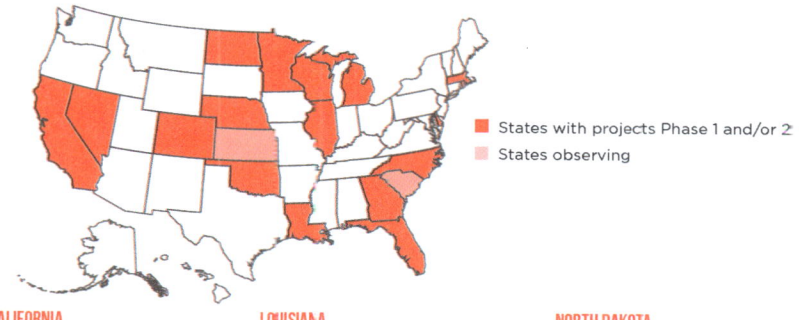

■ States with projects Phase 1 and/or 2
■ States observing

**CALIFORNIA**
Mapping

**COLORADO**
Monitoring, Paid leave, QI

**DELAWARE**
Medical-legal partnerships

**FLORIDA**
Monitoring, Place-based

**GEORGIA**
Montoring, Group Care

**ILLINOIS**
Assessment, Home visits

**KENTUCKY**
Mapping

**LOUISIANA**
Mapping

**MASSACHUSETTS**
Assessment, Taxes, Paid leave, Housing

**MICHIGAN**
Assessment

**MINNESOTA**
HEiAP, Assessment

**NEBRASKA**
Assessment, Monitoring, Mapping,
HEiAP, CLAS

**NEVADA**
Assessment, Place-based, ACEs

**NORTH CAROLINA**
Assessment, HEiAP

**NORTH DAKOTA**
ACEs, Monitoring

**OHIO**
HEiAP, Fatherhood, Social networking

**OKLAHOMA**
QI

**RHODE ISLAND**
HEiAP, Place-based, ACEs

**WISCONSIN**
Assessment, Taxes, Justice

SOUTH CAROLINA

KANSAS

WHO Framework for Tackling Social Determinants of Health and Infant Mortality
CoIIN SDOH Recommended Strategies, 0215-17

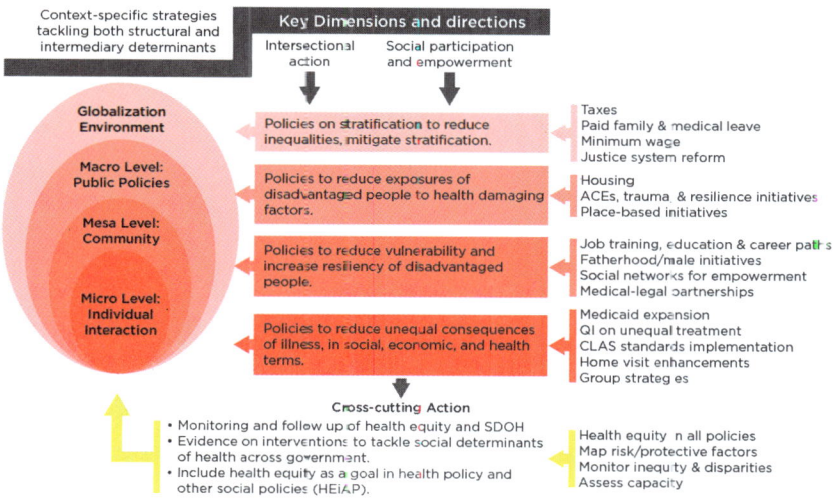

**FIGURE 6.1. Tackling Social Determinants of Health using Existing Programs**

*The Social Determinants of Health Learning Group from IM CoIIN built upon the efforts of others rather then reinventing programs and policies for maternal child health. The Infant Mortality CoIIN Prevention Toolkit allows users to learn interactively from states' experiences. IM CoIIN's approach to tackling SDH can be generalized to help communities address more than infant mortality. The World Health Organization recommends communities use a similar approach to address many medical issues influenced by social determinants of health, including: obesity, opiate epidemic, healthy aging, racism, education reform, reproductive justice, binge drinking, gun violence, suicide, pollution, and unsafe neighborhoods. By applying evidence-based programs and policies to address the upstream drivers of disease, we will promote health and prevent harm where our families live, work, learn, and play. Source: SDOH Learning Network Core Team: Co-chairs Alethia Carr and Kay Johnson; Jeanette Kowalik, Association of Maternal and Child Health Programs; and Vanessa Lee; Maternal and Child Health Bureau, Health Resources and Services Administration, US HHS. September, 2017.*

Both preventing and addressing unmet social needs will require system redesign, planning, a motivated workforce, and engaged families. All of these are best addressed locally, in the home, the workplace, and the community. The best use of your first $5,000 as a community is to align existing programs and policies to address the upstream drivers of health and disease: the social determinants of health. It costs very little to enhance existing programs and coordinate current work on priority population health issues. Previous reforms have failed to focus on the heart of the population health problem: how can we support a healthy community using existing programs and policies?

| NAME | INITIATING SECTOR | COMMUNITY STAKEHOLDERS | APPROACH | FOCUS | FUNDERS | WEBSITE |
|---|---|---|---|---|---|---|
| 100 MILLION HEALTHIER LIVES | Nonprofit | Health care, Public Health and other sectors working to improve health | Help 100 million people live healthier lives by 2020, fundamentally transform the way the world thinks and acts to improve health, well-being and equity to get breakthrough results | Public Health/ Health care | RWJF with Institute for Health care Improvement | http://www.100mlives.org |
| ACTIVE LIVING BY DESIGN | Philanthropy | Public Health, Public Policy, Urban Planning, Design, Community Development, Architecture, Social Work, Nutrition | Creates community-led change by working with local, state, and national partners to build a culture of active living and healthy eating | Public Health/ Health care | RWJF with Third Sector New England | http://activeliving-bydesign.org |
| ALIGNMENT OF HEALTH EQUITY AND DEVELOPMENT (AHEAD) | Nonprofit | Community Development, Public Health, Health care | Aligns resources of health and community development stakeholders to improve health | Community Development | Public Health Institute, Reinvestment Fund, Kresge Foundation | http://www.alignhealthequity-develop.org |
| BRIDGING FOR HEALTH | Nonprofit | Health Care, Public Health, Social Services, Business, Schools, Housing and others | Improves population health by rebalancing and aligning investments while fostering linkages among public health, health care and other sectors | Public Health/ Health care | RWJF with technical support from Georgia Health Policy Center | http://ghpc.gsu.edu/project/bridging-for-health/ |
| BUILDING HEALTH PLACES NETWORK | Nonprofit | Community Development, Public Health, Health care | Catalyzes and supports collaboration across the community development and health sectors to improve low-income communities and lives of people living in them. | Community Development | RWJF with Public Health Institute | http://www.build-healthyplaces.org |
| COMMUNITIES JOINED IN ACTION | Nonprofit | Public health, Health care | Creates networks of community health collaborative to improve access and eliminate disparities | Public Health/ Health care | RWJF with Georgia Health Policy Center | http://www.cjaonline.net |
| COUNTY HEALTH RANKINGS AND ROADMAPS | Philanthropy | Public Health, Business, Education, Philanthropy, Investors, Nonprofits, Community Development, Government and Health care | Strengthens capacity to advance efforts to build a Culture of Health for their communities | Community Development | RWJF | http://www.countyhealthrank-ings.org |

| | | | | | | |
|---|---|---|---|---|---|---|
| **MOVING HEALTH CARE UPSTREAM** | Academic Institution | Health care | Accelerate innovations that improve health of the community by promoting child and family well-being | Public Health/ Health care | Kresge Foundation | http://moving-health careup-stream.org |
| **NETWORK FOR REGIONAL HEALTH CARE IMPROVEMENT** | Nonprofit | Health care, Public Health | Improves health and health care in communities across the U.S. through an active and engaging Regional Health Improvement Collaborative | Public Health/ Health care | RWJF | http://www.nrhi.org |
| **PLAN4HEALTH** | Government, Nonprofit | Local Government (Planning, Public Health) | Support creative partnerships to build sustainable, cross-sector coalitions (focus on increasing health equity through nutrition or physical activity) | Local Government | CDC, American Public Health Association, American Planning Association | http://plan4health.us |
| **SPREADING COMMUNITY ACCELERATORS THROUGH LEARNING AND EVALUATION (SCALE)** | Nonprofit | Public Health (health depart-ment), health care (insurers and hospitals), community based organizations, education | Assists communi-ties to achieve unprecedented results in improving the health and well-being of people, populations and community-at-large and to close equity gaps | Public Health/ Health care | RWJF with 100 Million Healthier Lives and Institute for Health care Improvement | |
| **WHAT WORKS CITIES** | Philanthropy | Local govern-ment (public health, afford-able housing, transportation, planning, public safety) | Help 100 mid-sized American cities enhance their use of data and evidence to improve services, inform local decision-making and engage residents | Local Government | Bloomberg Philanthropy | https://whatwork-scities.bloomberg.org |

 **TABLE 6.2. Capacity Building Network that Support Local Population Health Collaborations**

## REFLECTION QUESTIONS

1. If you wanted to try and align community effort, then what would good look like in your neighborhood, town, or county?

2. Try to place a population health program within an aligning community effort framework. Grade your program by each dimension:

   □ Smart implementation (including geography, priority population, identification and screening, navigation and resource connection, team, and workflow)

   □ Good governance (data and evaluation, community partnerships, leadership, and financing)

3. What would be the benefits (and challenges) that might accelerate (or prevent) your attempts to align community effort? How would you explain your plan to your next-door neighbor?

---

**PART 6 ENDNOTES**

1   Health Leads, https://healthleadsusa.org

PART 7

# COLLABORATION ON HEALTH

**CHALLENGE:** Will collaboration on health accelerate improvement in population health outcomes?

How do you move from complaining about a problem to working toward a solution? Everyone has his or her favorite complaint about community collaborations. Urban Dictionary defines *collaboration* as:

*an unnatural act practiced by nonconsenting adults*

*Worker A: "We have no common interests. We don't like each other. And it irritates us to work together. But we were told by management to work together.*

*Worker B: [sigh!] Let's start collaborating.*

Even when organizations want to work together, there many examples of collaboration leading to "the kinds of transactions," as explained by the *Devil's Dictionary*, "in which *A* plunders from *B* the goods of *C*, and for compensation *B* picks the pocket of *D* of money belonging to *E*." The end result is that resources, time, and money are wasted purchasing *X* goods that the community didn't really need or want for *Y* price that the stakeholders individually could never afford. So a cynic might conclude, "There are so many reasons that collaboration hasn't worked and doesn't work . . . why are we still talking about collaborating?"

Heidi Gardner has researched collaboration in a very rigorous way for the last decade. Author of the book *Smart Collaboration: How Professionals and Their Firms Succeed by Breaking Down Silos*, Gardner is an expert on collaboration. In her article "How to Capture Value from Collaboration, Especially If You're Skeptical About It," she notes:

> Teamwork all too often feels inefficient (search and coordination costs eat up time), risky (can I trust others to deliver for my client?), low value (our own area of expertise always seems most critical), and political (a sneaky way of self-promoting to other areas of one's firm). Lurking behind these reservations may be concerns about losing relevance, becoming . . . "all form, no substance."[1]

Collaboration does not happen easily or by accident. Collaboration on health means that stakeholders—health systems, public health, social services, business, and philanthropy—work together to create a new, better community. Rather than just focusing on the end ideal—trust leads to shared risks, shared costs, shared success—we can consider the continuum from competition—the status quo—toward collaboration with multiple positive, productive steps between where we start and where we want to go.

How do you change your mindset so that you are working with a positive impact, delivering good programs to more people and systematically tackling the greatest challenges in your community?

## COLLABORATION IS DIFFICULT

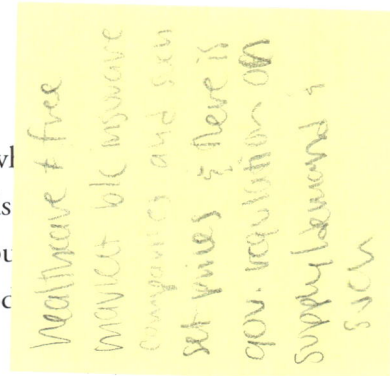

Basic health economics helps explain wh

Without getting too far into the weeds

"basic notions of health economics" pu

Michael Drummond and Gregory Stoc

cians to health policy:

- Human wants are unlimited and resources are finite.

- Health economics is as much about benefits as it is about costs.

- Many of the simple rules of free markets do not apply in the case of healthcare.

- The provision of healthcare is but one way of improving the health of the population.

- As a community, we prefer to postpone costs and to bring forward benefits.

- Equity in healthcare may be desirable, but reducing inequalities usually comes at a price.[2]

Taken together, these basic assumptions about health economics help explain the gap between what we want—low-cost, effective population health solutions implemented at scale in our community—and what we see—fragmented, duplicative systems that frustrate providers and fail to improve the health and well-being of working families. I would argue that there exists a metaphorical activation energy that community organizations must overcome before they can effectively and efficiently collaborate.

## TYPES OF INTERACTIONS WHEN ORGANIZATIONS
## WORK ON THE SAME PROBLEM

Interactions between organizations can be characterized on a continuum from competing to collaborating. Not all organizations are direct competitors; not every community has organizations that are willing to collaborate on population health priorities. It is important to think about the history of your community and how organizations have managed to succeed or fail when they try to collaborate. Let's look at how different types of interactions between organizations influence population health.

There are times and situations where competition may be preferable to collaboration. In a free market where rational agents make informed decisions with perfect understating of cost, risk, and benefits, then competition could lead to the optimal outcome. However, population health is not an optimized free market. Healthcare systems are highly regulated. Pricing is not transparent. The cost of goods and services exceeds the purchasing power of individuals, leading to the third-party purchasing problem. In addition, there is a significant time lag between exposures and outcomes, which encourages individuals to skip effective prevention measures until adverse outcomes develop, leading to more expensive, crisis-oriented interventions. Competition can be good, healthy, and optimal in certain situations—but population health is not one of them.

In college, I worked as a general chemistry teacher assistant. I ran the general chemistry lab—fire, acid, and explosions made to educate and entertain—and the weekly review sessions. One topic that I loved teaching was the idea of Activation Energies. The activation energy is the minimum energy that must be available to a chemical system for potential reagents to result in a chemical reaction. In terms of collaboration, *activation energy* is the minimum amount of effort, time, and resources required to transition from a current status quo to a future state where health outcomes are improved, waste is eliminated, and workers are productive.

As we think about population health, it is important to think about inputs—time, energy, effort, and resources—and results—health outcomes, community expenses, and cost-savings. I find it useful to picture the competition, coexistence, communication, cooperation, coordination and collaboration on a spectrum.

## POPULATION HEALTH SPECTRUM

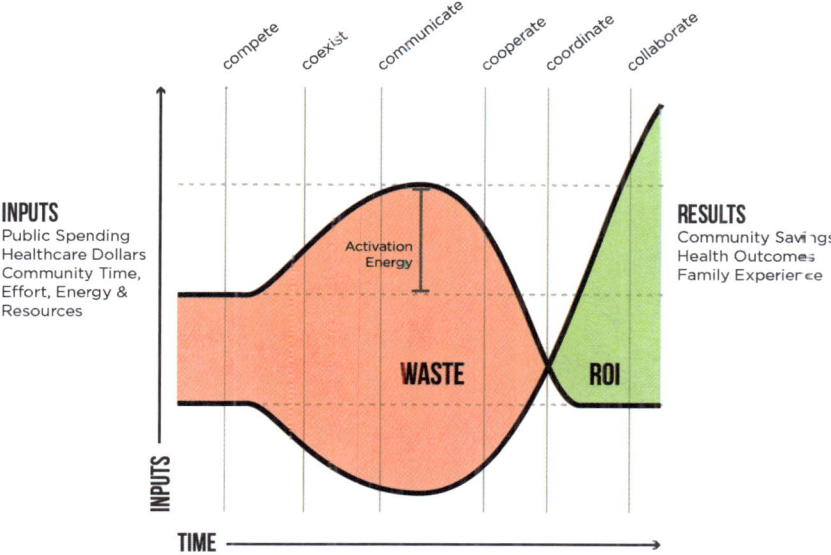

**FIGURE 7.1. From Competition to Collaboration: The Benefits, Challenges, and Intermediate Stages**

*I visualize the benefits, challenges, and intermediate stages between competition and collaboration like a chemical reaction. When organizations compete, community resources are wasted on redundant, not aligned activities. The process of communicating, cooperating, and coordinating requires time, energy, effort, and money. Many communities find that the intermediate stages preceding community collaboration are more expensive and less productive than simple competition. Yet, communities who collaborate* may uncover a substan[...] individual, [...] ties collabor[...]   The benefit of aligned effort is that [...] and less expensive when communities [...] lth priorities.

[handwritten note: Competition in MC = wasted resources < poor results]

It is h[...] ce between the black line (inputs) and [...] productivity across the community. [...] ivity as the difference between resu[...] 's positive when results exceed inputs, [...] results fall short of inputs. When everyone comp[etes], the consequence is wasted resources and poor results. At the end of the day, money is spent, time effort is expended, and results don't change. The only thing worse than competition is situations where organizations coexist or communicate but fail to trust one another.

Organizational coexistence leads to fragmentation and duplication of efforts (more inputs), but may actually waste time and energy of families, leading to confusion, frustration, and poor follow-through. As a consequence, results get worse. Communication is a key step to overcoming the activation energy required to move from a state of competition to a new state of community collaboration. Organizations that communicate have access to more funds, resources, and opportunities, particularly if they are able to pursue and obtain outside funding. However, the grant cycle is slow, time consuming, resource intensive, and time limited. Short-term funding (grants) can lead to investments in better population health, but may pull organizations away from their core strengths and mission in the pursuit of funder's priorities. As organizations are stretched thin, they may start to ask for help and be willing to offer help. But the immediate changes in workforce, services, and community activities may not ultimately improve the health and well-being of families.

It is only when multiple community organizations are cooperating that we see community results improve. This is a common "danger zone" for community activities. At this point, the allocation of time, energy, and resources is more than at baseline (competition status quo), and though results are improving it is very difficult to assign responsibility to the success. In addition, cooperation is often more expensive for individual community agencies due to time, resources, and effort required to cooperate between agencies, pulling staff away from serving clients.

The likely next step, in absence of trust, shared vision, and leadership, is a reversion to the status quo. Organizations begin to squabble over credit, and partnerships break down. When communities are able to push through and begin to cooperate, then results begin to dramatically improve. Organizations that partner together, work well together, and integrate services in a comprehensive, proactive manner will begin to see results exceeding their investments. Population health efforts begin to shine when communities collaborate.

⌈In a true collaboration, every organization is working to its productive capacity, work is shared, overhead is low and distributed across stakeholders, no efforts are duplicated, and the common infrastructure provides a strong foundation for innovation, scaling up successful projects, adapting to challenges, and measurably improving the health and well-being of the community.⌋

It is important to the think critically about the opportunities and risks at each stage of the transition from competition to collaboration.

## PHASES IN A TRANSITION FROM COMPETITION TO COLLABORATION

| INTERACTIONS BETWEEN ORGANIZATIONS | MOVING FROM COMPETITION TOWARDS COLLABORATION | | | COLLABORATION SPECTRUM | | |
|---|---|---|---|---|---|---|
| | **COMPETE** | **COEXIST** | **COMMUNICATE** | **COOPERATE** | **COORDINATE** | **COLLABORATE** |
| **DESCRIPTION** | Competition for clients, resources, partners and public attention | No systematic connection between agencies. | Open to information sharing or networking | As needed, short-term, often informal, interactions on discrete activities or projects | Organizations systematically adjust and align work, establish formal relationships, and share division of roles | Durable, long term relationships between partners based on shared mission, goals, decision-making, resources |
| **TRUST OF POTENTIAL PARTNERS** | **Distrust**— information is viewed as a competitive advantage | **Guarded**— open to unidirectional relationships where others share resources or clients | **Ask for help**— use information collected by others, but doubts quality of outside information | **Listen**— use information from other to improve services, and shares information with partners | **Partner**— sphere of common interest that benefits clients. Partners shared resources and rewards. Increased tolerance for risk | **Trust**— fully integrated programs, planning, funding and public attention. Greater risk as partners jointly secure resources and share rewards. |
| **ORIENTATION TOWARDS POTENTIAL PARTNERS** | **Defensive**— fiercely defend turf and attack perceived threats | **Tolerant**— view all other community efforts as unrelated | **Seeks Help**— tries to use other organizations to facilitate internal growth | **Join Forces**— get together with other organizations in community-wide initiatives | **Work Well Together**— Organizations prioritize individual strengths and coordinate with partners to address weaknesses | **Sharing Risk and Rewards**— infrastructure and overhead in common - invest in each other to improve client outcomes |
| **INTEGRATION OF SERVICES AND STRATEGY** | Non-existent- Inconsistent with Strategy | | | **Partial**— clients may utilize services at multiple organizations on a limited basis | **Comprehensive**— referral systems with open channels of communication and shared resources. | **Complete**— tight integration between organizations. Clients needs are fully supported through collective planning and well-defined channels of communication. |
| **MISSION, VISION AND GOVERNANCE** | | | | Independent authority, Separate Resources, but Shared Vision | Separate authority and power may be an issue, but shared mission and rewards allow for longer-term interactions around a specific effort | Structure determines authority as separate organizations realign with full commitment to a common mission, vision and governance model. |

*adapted from Stanford Social Innovation Review. Collective Impact (2014) and Management Academy for Public Health, http://sph.unc.edu/nciph/maph (2006)

**TABLE 7.1 Type of interacations between Community Agencies Interested in Population Health**

# COMPETE

When community stakeholders compete on population health, they each strive to gain either by defeating or by establishing superiority over others.

In highly competitive fields, organizations compete for clients, resources, partners, and public attention. Organizations are unlikely to trust potential partners, and information is viewed as proprietary—a competitive advantage to be hoarded. When organizations compete for a scarce economy, it is easy to adopt a defensive posture and to attack perceived threats. This creates a hostile environment where it is impossible to integrate services and strategy—even in areas where integration might benefit the client, organization, and community.

It is easy to assume that businesses would be the organizations most likely to compete on population health. However, it is rarely true that you find too many for-profit ventures fighting to own population health programs. The benefits of population health are distributed throughout the community. However, the investments are made up front, requiring large amount of time, energy, effort, and funding, and always involve significant risk to stakeholders. Though business may bear the brunt of the costs of a sick community—both through lost productivity of workers and higher insurance premiums—they are downstream from the direct beneficiaries of community investment: namely, working families, local government, and healthcare payers.

The most competitive organizations are often small nonprofits and large integrated healthcare systems. It is true: a small nonprofit may function on a budget of thousands of dollars. But small organizations are lean, agile, inventive, innovative, and not constrained by shareholders demanding a financial ROI every quarter. I have started three successful nonprofits that worked under-the-radar to improve the health and well-being of vulnerable populations. The staff at non-profits are typically paid less (or paid ____ an a comparable position at a private ____ s are often influenced by external fac ____ and funder preferences. Funding ofte ____ me-lined grants that do not ebb and fl ____ t is also difficult to compare the succes ____ Leaders of non-profits end up scrambl ____ ntial programs and trying to out-hustl ____ e street.

Large integrated h ____ systems, on the other hand, have budgets in the billions. It is not uncommon for a healthcare system to write off $200 million dollars a year in uncompensated expenses. However, healthcare system growth opportunities are limited by the size of the insured population who lives in their catchment area. I did my public health training in Boston, a healthcare mecca. Within one mid-sized US city—population 650,000—there were four healthcare systems with annual operating budgets exceeding a billion dollars. With multiple systems competing for the attention of potential patients and funding from the federal government, fragmentation, duplication, and waste were inevitable. The competition between healthcare systems was fierce, especially for paying patients. Before the Affordable Care Act, there was no incentive for hospitals to collaborate. Plus, the regulations on patient information gave hospitals legal rationales NOT to integrate systems and share patient data. In a cut-throat, competitive environment, concession to public good made in the name of "population health" were as likely to be corporate strategy designed to turn an adversary's ill-conceived advance into a sunk-cost endeavor as it was to result improved health and well-being for working families.

It is very hard—if not impossible—to measure population health when organizations compete instead of collaborate. In communities dominated by organizations that compete against one another, it will be very difficult to impact population health outcomes. The best you can hope for is that organizations working in similar areas will manage to coexist.

## COLLABORATE

Collaboration is more effective at achieving population health at scale than competition. Collaboration is a way of working that attracts and involves people outside one's formal control, organization, and expertise to accomplish common goals. Now, partner organizations are taking on long-term projects based on shared mission, goals, decision-making, and resources. The organizations are now co-dependent. They are now willing to sacrifice self-sufficiency for great efficacy. This is risky. It is scary. But it is an essential step to transforming systems, changing culture, and improving population health.

Collaboration requires trust. In his landmark book *First Things First*, Steven Covey makes the point that trust—or a lack of trust—is the rate-limiting step that drives, or inhibits, productivity. "Trust is the glue that holds everything together," notes Covey and he continues:

> It creates the environment in which all of the other elements— win-win stewardship agreements, self-directing individuals and teams, aligned structures and systems, and accountability—can flourish.[3]

Collaboration is the state where fully integrated programs allow for infrastructure and overhead in common. Community organizations invest in each other to improve population health outcomes. Frontline workers are rewarded for efforts outside of the organization and in the community.

Integration is now complete. There are tightly coupled pathways between organizations. Protocols are shared and inter-dependent. A client's needs are fully supported. Personal data is shared, protected, and valued as a resource that is stewarded across the community, but not owned or hoarded by any one organization.

There are multiple national and regional organizations that can help your community learn to collaborate. You don't have to navigate community collaboration blindly. There exists many national and regional organizations that provide support to communities seeking to improve population health outcomes.

Heidi Gardner makes the point that if you want to capture value from collaboration, it is not enough to *know* about collaboration, you have to *practice* collaborating on a regular basis. Smart collaboration is a skill that you will hone, refine, and develop with time. She says:

> *It's one thing to acknowledge the value of collaboration intel-*
> *lectually; it's another to internalize its potential so fully that*
> *you proactively seek more collaboration opportunities and*
> *that collaborative skills become central to your professional*
> *identity. Neither the true benefits of collaboration nor the*
> *required skill set adjustments, however, become apparent*
> *until you've made a go of it.*[4]

Rather than providing materials or webinars, a good capacity-building network will provide on-the-ground instruction, practical know-how, and a learning community that will share with your collaboration. There is no one right national capacity-building network. But the variety of organizations means that you will have many, many tools and examples to build from if you are just starting to collaborate. In addition, the organizers tend to be open to inquiries and are willing to share tips on where to start and how to connect. I would also recommend that you keep an eye out for webinars, conferences, and networking events. There are tons of opportunities to get more involved.

## WHY IS COLLABORATION SO HARD?

Population health issues are insidious at present, and disastrous in the future. Leaders must balance short-term expenses against highly uncertain future costs. A healthy community that promotes measurable and efficient collaboration between healthcare, public health, and social services has been almost impossible to create and even more difficult to sustain. Our population health problem is compounded by the multifactorial nature of the social determinants of health, which defy simple cause–effect explanations. Social determinants are all the knotty, difficult-to-untangle drivers of health and disease. As we have discussed, addressing any one social determinant—such as housing insecurity—also involves tackling unemployment and adult education, which assumes solutions to problems of childcare, transportation, and financial hardship. But we really can't begin to address financial hardship until all our community members have access to safe, affordable housing—a housing-first approach. If we can address all the unmet needs at once, and continually re-assess at-risk families for challenges and setbacks, then we can make progress toward our goal of a just society with equitable health outcomes for all families at lower cost to healthcare systems, government, and businesses.

## Common Biases May Confound Attempts to Collaborate

Four cognitive biases that make population health especially challenging include: Confirmation Bias, Optimism Bias, Instant Gratification, and Loss Aversion. Together, these four examples of broken decision-making make collaboration more difficult.

## Confirmation Bias

**Confirmation bias**: a tendency to interpret new evidence as confirmation of our existing beliefs or theories.

The issue of collaboration on population health issues has been polarizing and highly politicized. We live in a time of social media, personalized news feeds on Facebook, talk show hosts, Twitter, and cable news networks that tend to reinforce our existing beliefs. This leads to confirmation bias, which drives us to seek out information that is consistent with our existing views, rather than data that may challenge or refute those views. Instead of looking for information for the sake of gaining more knowledge, we look for information that supports our established opinions.

However, collaboration requires curiosity. We need to overcome confirmation bias, to be seeking out opinions, ideas, facts, and proposals that challenge our assumptions. Curiosity can help us overcome confirmation bias.

## Optimism Bias

**Optimism bias**: a belief that I—as opposed to someone who looks, acts, or lives differently from me—am at a lesser risk of experiencing a negative event.

We are all at risk of getting sick. We can study risk, stratify risk, manage risk, and event reduce risk. But risk is always present. The fact that I was not sick yesterday does not mean that I will not get sick tomorrow, next week, or next year. Optimism bias blinds decision-makers to real-world scenarios—especially negative events—and leads to population health planning based on illogical predictions of sunny skies every day. When we envision how our community will look a generation from now, we see it through rose-colored glasses. We don't picture faltering businesses or abandoned neighborhoods, or imagine a family in bankruptcy due to unpaid medical bills. In the same way, when we picture the plight of poor families in the United States, we can imagine that we—as a society—will address those unmet social needs—transportation, child care, housing, employment, education, financial security, friendship—in a timely, transparent, and effective way. The social needs appear to be so basic that it is hard to imagine that a wealthy society abounding in resources such as ours could not take care of every man, woman, and child.

Base rates help us to overcome optimism bias. We can measure risk, and we can quantify the likelihood that particular events will occur. These base rates—such as how often important events occur in the community—are strong predictors of population health outcomes. But base rates keep us grounded in reality and prevent optimism bias from hijacking common sense.

## Instant Gratification

**Instant gratification**: the desire to experience pleasure without delay or deferment. → pop. health takes time

It is really hard to work hard now so that we will benefit in the future. Showing restraint and exercising self-control is difficult to do—especially when the payoff isn't immediate. We all encounter this every day, when we decide what to eat or how to spend our money.

The famous Stanford marshmallow experiment highlighted the bias toward instant gratification: children were given a marshmallow and told they either could eat it immediately or wait fifteen minutes and get a second marshmallow. Most ate the single one immediately; interestingly, it was found that those who waited tended to do better later in life.[5] Energy projects and large-scale population health initiatives present a similar dilemma on the loss side: [despite significant payoffs down the road, the immediate cost and necessary sacrifices are a major deterrent.]

Positive peer pressure and focusing on specific future outcomes helps us overcome our natural inclination toward instant gratification. Friends and partners keep us accountable. A shared vision for a specific, concrete population health achievement keeps us motivated, and a tracking our progress keeps us accountable. Peer pressure—like participating in a team or a group—can be a strong motivator for positive change in the community.

Ben Hecht is the CEO of *Living Cities,* an organization that harnesses the collective knowledge from foundations and banks to benefit the urban poor. The goal of Living Cities is to re-engineer obsolete public systems so as to connect people to opportunity. Ben's experience has taught him:

> *Collaboration can be messy and time consuming. From the very beginning, you must develop clarity of purpose and artic-ulate, "What can we do together that we could not do alone?" Often, this means thinking beyond individual projects to whole solutions and big, bold ideas.*[6]

The focus on a specific future outcome—"What can we do together that we could not do alone?"—helps to overcome the bias of instant gratification and focus efforts on the long-term wins that can only be achieved through sustained collaboration.

## Loss Aversion

**Loss aversion**: a tendency to prefer avoiding losses over equivalent gains.

A fear of failure protects the status quo and makes us nervous to try new ideas, even when we know the old way does not work. Rather than taking a more rational expected utility approach to risk, and paying the small upfront loss to avoid future disaster, people will often gamble and hope for the best. Politicians are further reluctant to incur significant economic losses in the short term to due to re-election pressures, even though it will take years of sustained effort to address climate change or our population health crisis.

Behavioral science expert and Nobel Prize winner Daniel Kahneman describes an experiment in his book *Thinking Fast and Slow*. He gives a clear example of loss aversion. People were asked if they would accept a bet based on the flip of a coin. If the coin came up tails, the person would lose $100, and if it came up heads they would win $200. The results of the experiment showed that, on average, people needed to gain about twice (1.5x–2.5x) as much as they were willing to lose in order to proceed with the bet.

Collaboration on population health is difficult because it takes more inputs—while achieving worse results—to coexist, to communicate, and to cooperate than it does to compete. But it is a big hurdle for a community to jump directly from competition to collaboration. We need to learn to trust each other first.

One strategy for addressing loss aversion is to distribute risk across a number of stakeholders. It is possible to spread the cost of failure across a group. In some ways, it is easier to deal with less if we can normalize it, generalize it, and share it as a community. It is important to view population health as a number of small risks aggregated together. Many people would hesitate before accepting Kahneman's lose $100 but win $200 coin flip. But a wise person might respond: "I won't bet because I would feel the $100 loss more than the $200 gain. But I'll take you on if you promise to let me make 100 bets." Population health is a long game; communities that take a broad view of risk continue to invest in health will be the towns and counties that reap the rewards.

## WHY SHOULD WE COLLABORATE? BRAVING THE TRANSITION FROM COMPETITION TO COLLABORATION

Competition alone will never achieve the community transformation that lowers costs, delivers better services to families where they live, work and learn, and improves population health. Not all collaborations are smart. Collaboration involves messy, expensive, and risky work that crosses silos, specializations, roles, and traditional definitions of healthcare. Effective community collaboration can energize frontline workers, decrease risk for new population health initiatives, build shared infrastructure, create shared value, generate savings for stakeholders, and improve the health and well-being of families across the community. In the end, collaboration means getting stuff done that could not be done in any other way but through sustained, connected efforts.

## REFLECTION QUESTIONS

1.   What is the most valuable service in your organization? How could you make your most valuable product or

service better through community collaboration? If you don't know, find out. If you do know, then ask your customers—the community—if you are delivering.

2.  How can you alter the reward structure of your organization to reflect the reality that successful collaboration involves work outside of your organization?

3.  Take responsibility for the quality of information sharing in your community. How can you get the right information to the right people at the right time? Make a list of who you depend on for information and, in turn, who depends on you. How can you build trust with these people this week?

4.  Ben Hecht asks, "What can we do together that we could not do alone?" Draft a proposal to turn a single organization social effort into an opportunity for your community to collaborate. Do you need to start with a smaller goal—like to communicate, to cooperate, or to coordinate—or is your organization and your community ready to collaborate?

---

**PART 7 ENDNOTES**

1   Heidi Gardner and Herminia Ibarra, "How to Capture Value from Collaboration, Especially If You're Skeptical About It," *Harvard Business Review*, May 2, 2017, https://hbr.org/2017/05/how-to-capture-value-from-collaboration-especially-if-youre-skeptical-about-it

2   R. Cushman, M. Drummond, R. Labelle, G. Stoddart, "Health Economics: An Introduction for Clinicians," *Annals of Interior Medicine* 107, no. 1, July 1, 1987.

3   Steven Covey and Roger Merrill, "First Things First," *Franklin Covey Publishing*. 1994.

4   Heidi Gardner and Herminia Ibarra, "How to Capture Value from Collaboration, Especially If You're Skeptical About It," *Harvard Business Review*, May 2, 2017, https://hbr.org/2017/05/how-to-capture-value-from-collaboration-especially-if-youre-skeptical-about-it

5    Maria Konnikova, "The Struggles of a Psychologist Studying Self-Control,"
     *The New Yorker*, October 9, 2014, http://www.newyorker.com/science/
     maria-konnikova/struggles-psychologist-studying-self-control
6    Ben Hecht, "Collaboration is the New Competition," *Harvard Business Review*,
     January 10 2013, https://hbr.org/2013/01/collaboration-is-the-new-compe

PART 8

# POPULATION HEALTH GRAVEYARD

*"Population health is dying the death of a thousand pilots."*

—Quote taken from any public health
conference in the last ten years

**CHALLENGE:** Will your hometown collaboration escape the population health graveyard?

It is estimated that it takes an average of seventeen years to translate 14 percent of original research into benefit for patients, and an average of nine years for interventions recommended as evidence-based practices to be fully adopted.[1] The time between when researcher and innovators find a new, better way to improve population health and the day when the innovation is implemented in a local community is the Population Health Graveyard. There are many thousands of grant-funded projects and programs that never escape the population health graveyard. The Management Academy for Public Health (MAPH) was established to train state and local public health professionals to create revenue-generating public health programs. The primary goal of the ten-month MAPH training program was to enhance the operational effectiveness and efficiency of the state and local agencies through business planning. The outcome of interest was successful, sustainable, revenue-generating programs implemented at county health departments. Participants were trained to manage money, people, and data. Just to summarize the goal: the best teachers from public health and business working intensively with local county health leaders to accelerate local collaborations for health. What happened?

| ABILITY TO GENERATE ENHANCED REVENUE | | | |
|---|---|---|---|
| GENERATED ENHANCED REVENUE | NUMBER OF TEAMS | ENHANCED REVENUE | ENHANCED REVENUE PER TEAM |
| Yes | 28 (38.4%) | $6,045,359 | $215,906 |
| No | 45 (61.6%) | $0 | $0 |
| Total | 73 (100.0%) | $6,045,359 | $82,813 |

Teams able to implement revenue generating initiatives report raising an average of almost $216,000 each from a diverse mix of grant and fee-based funding streams. About two-thirds ($4.0 million) of the total enhanced revenue identified in this assessment is tied to existing initiatives.

 **TABLE 8.1. Success and Failure of County Health Departments to Create Revenue-Generating Programs**

*The Management Academy for Public Health trained and mentored teams at county*

*health departments to create revenue-generating public health programs. When teams were successful, they were wildly successful. After implementing a business plan, successful county health departments realized an additional $4 million dollars to improve community health. However, many county health departments struggled to implement business plans despite training and mentoring from the Management Academy of Public Health.*

The results were very exciting for public health leaders. Participating teams were able to generate revenue of almost $4 million, with an average of $215,000 new funds to address public health priorities after eighteen months. The return on investment was almost 3-to-1 for participants and funders. However, of the 118 teams who started the program, only 73 replied to the follow-up survey. Of the teams that completed the intensive, results-oriented program that focused on implementing programs at scale, only 38 percent of teams succeeded. In the end, 62 percent of public health business plans failed to generate revenue after eighteen months.[2] These pilot projects died in the population health graveyard.

## WHY DO POPULATION HEALTH COLLABORATIONS SUCCEED OR FAIL?

The reality is that successful population health collaborations are rare. Collaboration is difficult. Leading systems change is challenging. A lack of support from county health leadership, too few staff for the task, insufficient funds to overcome the activation energy separating competition from collaboration, lack of time, and bad team dynamics kill collaboration. But collaboration is not impossible, and the benefits for communities that collaborate are measured in the hundreds of thousands of dollars of new revenue redirected to improve health and well-being.

## BECK'S MAP FOR NAVIGATING A MAZE

The London Underground is a public rapid transit system serving London. Opened in 1863, it is the world's oldest underground railway network, and one of the largest. It is also known for its iconic subway map, which has become the model for illustrating public transit networks in cities around the world. In 1931, Harry Beck had the idea of expanding this central area, distorting geography, and simplifying the map so that the railways appeared as straight lines with equally spaced stations. Ironically, Beck's initial proposal was rejected! However, he re-pitched his idea to the board two years later—and the rest is history.

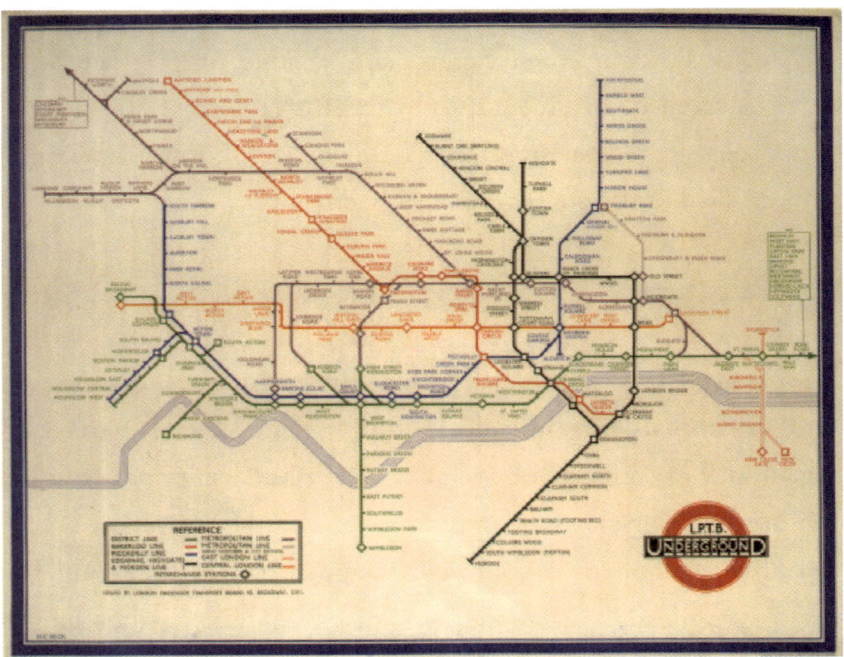

 **FIGURE 8.1. Harry Beck Redraws the London Underground**

*Harry Beck changed public transportation by making the London Underground map user friendly instead of geographically accurate. As one reporter explains, "Beck began by*

*replacing the map's existing sinuous curves with straight lines: horizontals, verticals, and forty-five-degree angles. He also skewed its scale, placing the stations at equal distances from one another, and removed the aboveground street grid. The result was a sparse, circuit board-like design that eschewed geographic accuracy for legibility." The result? Beck changed public transportation for the better. Source: The Verge (2013)*

Many population health collaborations work on the same principles as Harry Beck's map. Families need a subway map to help navigate the complicated healthcare, public health, and social service systems. Some services are offered within all three systems—but are called by different names. Other services are not offered except on a certain Tuesday if you happen to show up at the such-and-such desk or know this person's aunt who has an in with you-know-who. Population health collaborations expand the definition of health to include unmet social needs, distort healthcare-public health-social services to define solutions based on function not sector, and simplify the system so that families have clear pathways (straight lines) with ample advice for how to get from one station (behavioral health, transportation help, or child care) to another (housing or employment) until their final destination (quality education for their children or health insurance).

Imagine that the social determinants of health—instead of states of being—are places on a hypothetical map. Some of the problems—such as homelessness, unemployment, and transportation issues—would tend to cluster. Other advantages—such as safe neighborhoods, jobs, and good schools—might also tend to occur together. We can map the relationships between different social determinants of health like this:

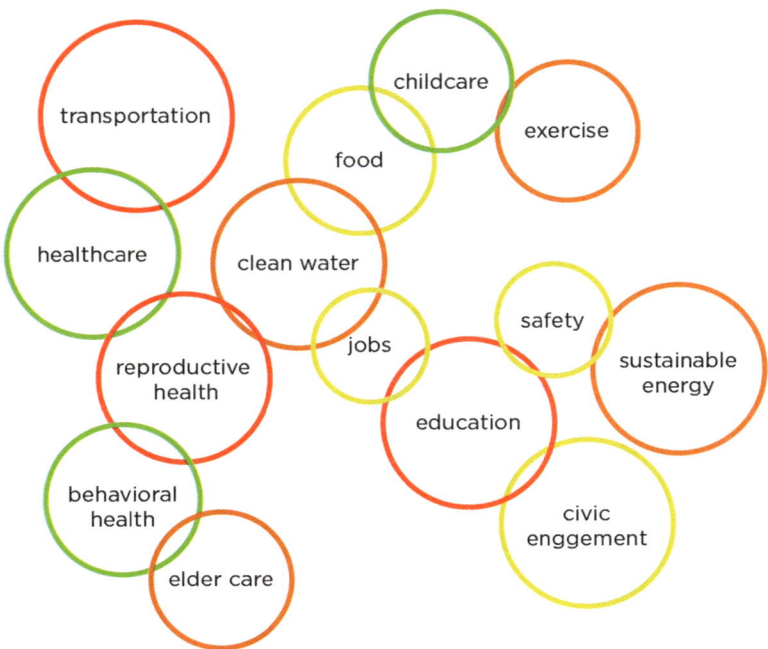

**FIGURE 8.2. Recognize the Upstream Drivers of Health and Disease—Diagram Relationships between Common Needs**

*It is important to highlight the relationships between social determinants of health when we consider community well-being. Many communities complete Community Health Needs Assessments. It is helpful to organize community needs by the various categories of health determinants: transportation, food, clear water, healthcare, reproductive health, behavioral health, exercise, tobacco use, energy use, jobs, childcare, education, elder care, civic engagement, and safety. There are issue-specific and neighborhood-specific clusters of disease drivers that can only be addressed to coordinated, community-wide efforts.*

The reality is that there are thousands of permutations for how a family might navigate the system. We don't need to standardize all the pathways, but we do need to provide clear signage to indicate "You are here!" and guide maps to help individuals reach their destination quickly, safely, and comfortably.

We need a map that looks like this:

**FIGURE 8.3. Pathways to Population Health: Map Resources across Sectors**

*There are many community agencies involved in building a healthy community. We can foster a shared vision for population health, collaborate on community programs, address the social determinants of health, and link social information to medical outcomes. However, a culture of health needs to be supported by clear, efficient connections between community agencies. Pathways to Population Health encourages communities to map resources across sectors and strengthen the links between programs.*

The figure is a metaphor, but like the Harry Beck's map, it can be extremely helpful. Population health clarifies the paths that an individual or an organization might pursue to improve the health of the community. Importantly, it connects individual needs, community services, and available funds to address basic needs quickly and efficiently.

Nirav Shah, MD MPH, is the senior vice president of Kaiser Permanente's Southern California region, a $24 billion health system with 14 hospitals, 168 medical offices, and more than 4 million members. Before joining Kaiser, he served as commissioner of the New York State Department of Health. He has served as a director for dozens of public and private institutions, received numerous NIH grants, and published more than one hundred peer-reviewed articles. When Kaiser launched its *Total Health* initiative to reach beyond the walls of the healthcare system and address unmet social needs of patients using community partnerships, Shah helped lead the effort. He was surprised to learn:

> *Of the 25,000 resources across 8 geographies in its database, just 1% of resources account for 50% of successful connections, and 10% of resources account for 90% of successful connections.*[3]

Just be encouraged that it is not necessary to find every single program that might, at some time, have benefited someone. Focus on the 10 percent of high-performing programs that help 90 percent of the community. The result is a metaphorical map that connects social factors to community resources.

**FIGURE 8.4. GRACE Redraws a Community: Connect Needs to Resources So Families Can Navigate Communities and Improve Health Outcomes**

When we gather resources and align community efforts, then we can address the social determinants of health and improve population health outcomes. GRACE works because it connects the needs of families with existing resources in the community. GRACE can help community leaders redraw the map, strengthen connections between community agencies, and simplify the process for families.

Dan Taylor, an innovative pediatrician in Philadelphia, acknowledges the need to gather resources to address social determinants of health in his community. He started an organization, Children's Advocacy Project or CAP4Kids Network, in 2005 as a way for healthcare providers, social workers, child advocates, and parents and teens to find reliable, up-to-date information on community resources.

CAP4Kids exists because most healthcare practitioners were not adequately prepared for, or had resources to turn to, for the many psychosocial, socioeconomic, and educational problems that faced many of their patients and families. It also came from the knowledge that there were many dedicated social service agencies in Philadelphia to serve those in need. The CAP was developed to bridge the gap between families in need and the social service agencies that serve them. Taylor notes:

> *The ultimate mission of The Children's Advocacy Project is to help bridge the gap between the many quality social service agencies in the area and the families that need their help the most. To bridge this gap, we aim to empower and to inform those that care for children and families through this web site. Cap4Kids will assist families, healthcare professionals, and social service providers by furnishing the tools necessary to connect families in need, to the appropriate social service agencies that serve them.*[4]

CAP4Kids hosts user-friendly websites that allow parents and families to find resources on a wide range of topics, ranging from after-school programs and camps, to education resources or resources for children with special needs. There are resources for pregnant mothers, infants, school-aged children, and teens. CAP4Kids has built websites for thirteen different communities, ranging in size and in geography from Miami to Hawaii, Philadelphia to Columbus. Dan is a visionary leader and thought clinician who saw the value in connecting common clinical problems related to food, shelter, childcare, and employment with experts and community resources.

When I wanted to find out what population health programs already existed in my community, I looked at a variety of sources. Taylor recommends:

*There are many different ways to gather content. Some cities have hardcopy or online listings of social service organizations in their locale. Some other resources are as follows: the United Way; the Division of Maternal and Child Health; Department of Human Services; 211 in selected cities; and social workers and parent advocates in your institutions.*

*Another effective way of gathering content is to perform online searches. Use search phrases such as "family services (city)," "child advocacy (city)," and more specific phrases such as "after-school programs (city)," "teen resources (city)." Then you can search various social service organizations, see if they list other sites on their website, request brochures, and start organizing.[5]*

I did the CAP4Kids method to map social resources and programs. Then the Population Health Underground looked at who was really addressing social needs for families. We found similar trends in La Crosse as Nirav Shav found with Kaiser. When we looked at the more than three hundred social needs programs—efforts addressing housing, nutrition, transportation, employment, adult education, safety, environmental health, and addiction—we found that social workers, information and referral specialists, and public health nurses routinely used the same forty-three programs as their first-line referral for clients with unmet social needs. The benefits of using existing programs to improve population health are many, but existing programs tend to have local champions, established funding mechanisms, a trained workforce, and low opportunity cost to leadership. If you build up existing programs, then you will have a better chance of escaping the population health graveyard.

# ESCAPING THE POPULATION HEALTH GRAVEYARD

There have been more than ninety models published for how to help local health leaders escape the population health graveyard. It is extremely difficult to move from a successful, grant-funded pilot to a sustainable population health program at scale. One of my favorite models is RE-AIM. RE-AIM is supported by a nationally recognized network of implementation scientists (re-aim.org) and has resulted in more than 720 peer-reviewed publications of health and public health programs.[6] It is an instructive framework to help local health leaders plan to collaborative.

RE-AIM is acronym that involves five key steps. By addressing each step individually, local health leaders can maximize their chances of escaping the population health graveyard:

1. **Reach**: the number who are *willing to participate* in a given initiative, intervention, or program.

2. **Efficacy**: the *impact of an intervention on outcomes*, including potential negative effects, quality of life, and economic outcomes.

3. **Adoption**: the number of *staff willing to initiate a program or policy in their setting*.

4. **Implementation**: fidelity to the various elements of an intervention's protocol. This includes *consistency of delivery* as intended and the time and cost of the intervention.

5. **Maintenance**: *systems change at six months* or institutionalization, *new* practice is now *routine* practice and policy.

At every step out of the population health graveyard, some programs will fail. Without a clear plan to improve adherence, the result of reaching seventy-five health departments with an evidence-based program at six months is one to two communities changed. The impact of an intensive, well-funded, well-staffed program like MAPH leads to twenty-six to twenty-eight programs changed. When communities use the RE-AIM approach, studies show they can achieve low-cost, effective results in one-in-five collaborations on population health. The advantage of coupling a strategy with existing programs, staff, and resources is that the opportunity cost for stakeholders is low, risk is spread across multiple agencies, and rewards—in both new financing, cost-saving, and improved health outcomes—can be substantial.

Every community's path to population health will look different, but the communities who gather resources and align community effort can expect similar benefits.

| ESCAPING THE POPULATION HEALTH GRAVEYARD: STEP-BY-STEP CHALLENGE FOR TRANSLATING COLLABORATION INTO PRACTICE | | | | |
|---|---|---|---|---|
| Goal: 75 County Health Departments (CHD) adopt County Health Implementation Plans (CHIP) to address Social Determinants of Health | | Coin Flip: 50% loss each step | Real World: % loss varies by step | RE-AIM: minimum 70% success each step |
| RE-AIM Concept | Step | % Loss (N=75) | | |
| Dissemination | County Health Kits disseminated to CHD | 50% (n=38) | 97% (n=73) | 97% (n=73) |
| Reach | CHD respond to County Kits | 50% (n=19) | 30% (n=22) | 80% (n=58) |
| Efficacy | CHD change CHIP to address SDH | 50% (n=9) | 60% (n=13) | 70% (n=40) |
| Adoption | CHD apply GRACE to accelerate system change | 50% (n=4) | 80% (n=10) | 80% (n=32) |
| Implementation | Evidence-based programs improve population health | 50% (n=2) | 40% (n=4) | 70% (n=22) |
| Maintenance | Counties to continue to save and reinvest 18 months later | 50% (n=1) | 50% (n=2) | 70% (n=16) |
| NUMBER OF COUNTY COLLABORATIONS THAT ESCAPE THE POPULATION HEALTH GRAVEYARD | | 1 | 2 | 16 |

**TABLE 8.2. Escaping the Population Health Graveyard: Step-by-Step**

## BREKKE CHALLENGE REVISITED: WOULDN'T IT BE GREAT TO HAVE A BILLION DOLLARS TO ADDRESS SOCIAL NEEDS?

Within your community lies a rich set of resources. In most cases, communities have only partially realized and tapped the potential of these resources for creating a better community. Applying the simple ideas and methods presented here can help you unleash this potential. Population health aims for evidence-based solutions to health problems reproduced at scale in your local community. It will help innovative programs to escape the population health graveyard. If you embrace population health as a shared vision for your community, then you will enhance existing programs, accelerate implementation of evidence-based practice, and help other communities by disseminating your results. As a result, we will be able to connect population health programs undertaken by communities all across the US.

There are opportunities for population health waiting to be discovered in your hometown. It was amazing what happened when frontline works from healthcare systems, Aging and Disability Resource Center, YMCA, the county health department, and the community-run free clinic worked together to enhance social needs programs in La Crosse. I want to see a thousand families receive a thousand dollars to address unmet social needs in a thousand counties. *Pathways to Population Health* has a bold vision for well-funded, high-functioning collaborations between healthcare, public health, social services, and nonprofits. When local stakeholders invest in building a healthy community, then we will see a billion dollars—1,000 x 1,000 x 1,000—mobilized to improve population health.

# REFLECTION QUESTIONS

1. What are the most pressing social needs in our community?

2. Who can we partner with?

3. How should your partnership measure our success?

---

**PART 8 ENDNOTES**

1   E.A. Balas, S.A. Boren, "Managing Clinical Knowledge for Healthcare Improvement," *Institute for Healthcare Improvement*, Yearbook of Medical Informatics, 65–70, 2000.
2   "Management Academy for Public Health: Final Program Evaluation," *J Public Health Management Practice*, Lippincott Williams & Wilkins, Inc., June 2003.
3   Michael Kanter, Artair Rogers, and Nirav Shah, "Healthcare that Targets Unmet Social Needs," *NEJM Catalyst*, April 13, 2016, http://catalyst.nejm.org/health-care-that-targets-unmet-social-needs/
4   The Children's Advocacy Project of America, http://cap4kids.org
5   Daniel Taylor, "CAP4Kids Implementation Manual," Children's Advocacy Project http://cap4kids.org
6   Reach, Efficacy, Adoption, Implementation, Maintenance, http://re-aim.org